£1-50

CW00956871

TRACING YOUR
SERVANT
ANCESTORS

FAMILY HISTORY FROM PEN & SWORD

Tracing Your Army Ancestors
Simon Fowler
•

Tracing Your Pauper Ancestors
Robert Burlison
•

Tracing Your Textile Ancestors
Vivien Teasdale
•

Tracing Your Railway Ancestors
Di Drummond
•

Tracing Secret Service Ancestors
Phil Tomaselli
•

Tracing Your Royal Marine Ancestors
Richard Brooks and Matthew Little
•

Tracing Your Jewish Ancestors
Rosemary Wenzerul
•

Fishing and Fishermen
Martin Wilcox
•

Tracing Your East Anglian Ancestors
Gill Blanchard
•

Tracing Your Ancestors
Simon Fowler
•

Tracing Your Liverpool Ancestors
Mike Royden
•

Tracing Your Scottish Ancestors
Ian Maxwell
•

Tracing Your Criminal Ancestors
Stephen Wade
•

Tracing Your Labour Movement Ancestors
Mark Crail
•

*Nick Barratt's Beginner's Guide to Your
Ancestors' Lives*
Nick Barratt
•

Tracing Your London Ancestors
Jonathan Oates
•

Tracing Your Shipbuilding Ancestors
Anthony Burton

Tracing Your Northern Irish Ancestors
Ian Maxwell
•

Tracing Your East End Ancestors
Jane Cox
•

Tracing the Rifle Volunteers
Ray Westlake
•

Tracing Your Legal Ancestors
Stephen Wade
•

Tracing Your Canal Ancestors
Sue Wilkes
•

Tracing Your Rural Ancestors
Jonathan Brown
•

Tracing Your Tank Ancestors
Janice Tait and David Fletcher
•

Tracing Your Family History on the Internet
Chris Paton
•

Tracing Your Medical Ancestors
Michelle Higgs
•

Tracing Your Second World War Ancestors
Phil Tomaselli
•

Tracing Your Channel Islands Ancestors
Marie-Louise Backhurst
•

Great War Lives
Paul Reed
•

The Territorials 1908–1914
Ray Westlake
•

Women's Lives
Jennifer Newby
•

Tracing Your Naval Ancestors
Simon Fowler
•

Family Matters
Michael Sharpe

TRACING YOUR SERVANT ANCESTORS

A Guide for Family Historians

Michelle Higgs

Pen & Sword
FAMILY HISTORY

First published in Great Britain in 2012 by
PEN & SWORD FAMILY HISTORY
an imprint of
Pen & Sword Books Ltd
47 Church Street
Barnsley
South Yorkshire
S70 2AS

Copyright © Michelle Higgs 2012

ISBN 978 1 84884 611 1

Typeset in Palatino and Optima by
CHIC MEDIA LTD

Printed and bound in England by
CPI Group (UK), Croydon, CR0 4YY

Pen & Sword Books Ltd incorporates the imprints of
Pen & Sword Aviation, Pen & Sword Maritime, Pen & Sword Military,
Wharncliffe Local History, Pen & Sword Select, Pen & Sword
Military Classics, Leo Cooper, Remember When,
Seaforth Publishing and Frontline Publishing

For a complete list of Pen & Sword titles please contact
PEN & SWORD BOOKS LTD
47 Church Street, Barnsley, South Yorkshire, S70 2AS, England
E-mail: enquiries@pen-and-sword.co.uk
Website: www.pen-and-sword.co.uk

CONTENTS

Contents

ACKNOWLEDGEMENTS

While writing this book, I received help and advice in locating information and illustrations from a number of different sources.

For this assistance, I would like to express my gratitude to the staff of Birmingham Archives and Heritage Service, Dudley Archives and Local History Service, and Lancashire Archives; and to Valerie Wardlaw of Falconer Museum, Forres.

I would also like to thank Alan Mackie and Carolyn Middleton who were so generous with their time and their research.

Finally, I would like to thank my husband Carl for his patience and support, and my family and friends for their encouragement during the writing of this book.

ILLUSTRATIONS

Every effort has been made to trace copyright holders of images included in this book. The publishers would be grateful for further information concerning any image for which we have been unable to trace a copyright holder.

INTRODUCTION

With more than 1.3 million domestic servants listed on the 1911 census, it is not surprising that many thousands of people today have a servant in their family tree. From the veritable army of staff kept by the gentry to service their country houses to the lowly 'maid of all work' employed by tradesmen and shopkeepers, there was a world of difference for the servant in terms of accommodation, wages and working conditions.

If you have an ancestor who was in domestic service, it is possible to find out more from general sources and specific servant-related records. However, the likelihood of finding your forebear in the sources depends to a large extent on when and where he or she lived and worked. Generally, you are more likely to find your ancestor if he or she was working in the mid- to late nineteenth century, or worked on a landed estate, or was sent into service by a poor law union or charitable organisation.

Even if you cannot find your forebear listed in any of the relevant sources, it is still possible to get a clearer picture of his or her working life from contemporary household manuals, and diaries and autobiographies of servants.

This book aims to give an overview of the role and places of work of domestic servants from the eighteenth century up to the Second World War. However, it will concentrate primarily on the nineteenth century as this was the heyday of the domestic servant. The book will look at the sources which can be used to trace those in service including printed records, original documents and some online sources.

In the bibliography, you will find the titles of more detailed publications about domestic service. The appendices include useful contacts listing relevant archives and libraries, as well as places to visit with servants' quarters.

Throughout the book, you will find case studies of real people who worked in domestic service. The sources section discusses a variety of records in greater detail, showing how they can be used to trace your own servant ancestor. This book assumes you have no previous knowledge of family history, but if you already know the basics of genealogical research, simply dip into the sections you are most interested in.

Part 1

DOMESTIC SERVICE

Chapter 1

DOMESTIC SERVICE THROUGH THE CENTURIES

The working-class origins of domestic servants in the Victorian era were almost unrecognisable from those who served in the castles and manors of the medieval period. At this time, men of gentle birth were routinely found among the upper servants in noble houses. According to Dorothy Marshall in *The English Domestic Servant in History*, this was because 'the belief that there was nothing degrading in performing even the most menial tasks for the well-born still held.' It was also still customary for young men 'of good social standing' to attend on the nobility as part of their training. Officials such as the clerk of the kitchen or the gentleman usher were carrying out tasks connected with running the domestic household which were similar to that of the later butler, but they were almost always well-bred.

After the turmoil of the English Civil War, great changes took place in formerly extravagant households. Aristocratic families had to adjust to a less costly way of life, and the new homes which were built were country estates rather than castles. The custom of sending young gentlemen into noble service died out around this time.

The roles of servants changed, with perhaps the steward being the only one to retain his important status, although he was usually no longer a gentleman by birth. The housekeeper took over the role of the clerk of the kitchen; the yeoman of the hall became the footman; the housemaid undertook tasks formerly carried out by the yeoman of the chamber; and the gentleman usher evolved into the butler.

The Seventeenth Century

Strikingly, from the mid-seventeenth century onwards, women were employed in domestic service in far greater numbers than in Tudor households. In addition, male servants were increasingly drawn from a lower social class than before.

Dorothy Marshall comments that the staff of a moderate seventeenth-century household was usually made up of 'a cook maid, a chamber maid or housemaid, possibly a waiting woman, a man-servant, and an odd boy'. When he began his famous diary in 1660, Samuel Pepys's household was less prosperous, having just one maid, Jane Birch. Jane had been employed by Pepys for three years when she left in August 1661. Samuel wrote: 'The poor girl cried, and I could hardly forebear weeping to think of her going; for though she be grown lazy and spoiled by Pall's [his sister] coming, yet I shall never have one to please us better in all things, and so harmlesse [sic], where I live.'

At this time, servants were an integral part of the household, often sleeping in their employer's bedrooms. Such intimacy led to strong personal relationships, and this was particularly the case with Jane Birch. She was a favourite of Samuel and his wife, and she returned to their service twice – in March 1662 for almost a year, and again in March 1666 until her marriage in March 1669 to Pepys's man-servant Tom Edwards.

By the end of 1664, Pepys's prospects and income had increased as had the number of servants he employed: 'My family is my wife, in good health, and happy with her; her woman Mercer, a pretty, modest, quiet maid; her chamber-maid Besse, her cook-maid Jane, the little girl Susan, and my boy, which I have had about half a year, Tom Edwards, which I took from the King's Chapel; and as pretty and loving quiet family I have as any man in England.'

The Eighteenth Century

In the early eighteenth century, servants were still considered as part of the family. Parson James Woodforde kept a cook/dairymaid, a housemaid, a footman, a boy and a farming man. In his diary, he writes about their illnesses, arguments and problems as one would refer to any family member.

The diary records numerous instances of kindnesses towards his staff, such as in 1776, when he paid the schoolmaster to 'teach my Servants Ben and Will to write and read at 4/6d a quarter each.' He took most of his servants to Norwich in 1783 to see a combined celebration of the recent peace and a saint's day 'as I was willing that all shd go that could. Betty, my Upper Maid stayed at home being Washing Week.' A year later, he recommended his own maid Lizzy for a place at Weston House, the nearest country estate.

In most cases, eighteenth-century households employed upper servants who were the offspring of farmers, artisans and labourers rather than reduced gentlemen. Black servants were a feature of the wealthiest households at this time, but were usually regarded as novelties by their masters and treated like overindulged pets, not as domestic servants. They did not normally undertake menial tasks.

A tax on male servants was first imposed in 1777 to help recoup the significant cost of the American War of Independence. Female servants were also taxed in 1785, but unsurprisingly, this move was extremely unpopular since it affected so many people, and families employing maids to help with their children were hardest hit. This taxation was repealed seven years later.

Hair powder, used by liveried footmen and coachmen, was also taxed between 1786 and 1869. Although the tax on male servants was eased during the nineteenth century, it was not finally abolished until 1937. This made male servants more expensive to employ than females, so they were traditionally only employed in the wealthiest of households.

The invention of a system of non-electric wire-operated bells in the Georgian era ushered in a period of change for domestic servants. Prior to this, it was necessary for a servant to be waiting in a room or just outside to be within earshot of his employer's voice or hand bell. Under the new system, the bells were usually positioned in a corridor or hall near the kitchen, with labels indicating which room required attention. This meant that servants could be summoned from a distance away and, according to Trevor May in *The Victorian Domestic Servant*, it 'was one of the factors that led to the increasing segregation of servants' quarters in larger houses.'

While the family had more privacy, for the servants it meant much toing and froing and endless interruptions to their daily chores. At the same time, the architecture of the new country houses, or those which had been remodelled, began to include separate servants' halls and staircases. The division between the servants' quarters and the family's on the ground floor was often by a door, which was fitted on the servants' side with green baize for soundproofing purposes.

The Nineteenth Century

In an age before washing machines, vacuum cleaners, central heating and hot running water, domestic servants were a necessity in large houses. In smaller nineteenth-century homes, the keeping of servants was a status symbol of the upwardly mobile middle classes.

THE "SERVICE" FRANCHISE.

JOHN THOMAS (loq.) "'ERE'S A PRETTY START, MISS MARIA! THEY'RE GOING TO GIVE GAMEKEEPERS AND SUCH-LIKE RUBBISH VOTES, AND HAC'SHALLY DON'T RECO'NISE US!!!"

'The Service Franchise', Punch, 15 March 1884

As John Burnett points out in *Useful Toil: Autobiographies of Working People from the 1820s to the 1920s*, 'the large family, the large and over-furnished house, the entertainment of guests at lavish dinner-parties, and the economic ability to keep one's wife in genteel idleness, all of which were essential attributes of the institution of the Victorian middle-class family, required the employment of servants on a vast scale.'

The phenomenon of the middle classes employing domestic servants mushroomed during the 1850s and 1860s, largely because until the end of the nineteenth century domestic help was cheap and plentiful.

At least one servant was kept by families with any kind of social pretensions. In Anthony Trollope's *Last Chronicle of Barset*, the impoverished curate Josiah Crawley was determined to keep a maid even though the furniture and carpets were visibly in need of repair. Keeping up appearances was vital to be counted in the Victorian social hierarchy, and it was important to be seen to have servants, so families employed as many as they could afford.

When undertaking his survey of poverty in York in 1899, Seebohm Rowntree took 'the keeping or not of domestic servants' as the dividing line between the working and middle classes. In York, the servant-keeping classes amounted to around 30 per cent of the population. However, as Trevor May argues in *The Victorian Domestic Servant*, this view ignored the fact that 'many artisans and other members of the working class employed domestic help (to act as child-minders, wash clothes or do "the rough") and that even some of these servants lived in.'

The census provides some interesting statistics about the growth in numbers of domestic servants. In 1851, there were almost one million domestic servants in Britain, only dwarfed by the number of people employed in agriculture (which included farm servants).

By 1881 the number of females in resident domestic service had increased to 1,230,406, but twenty years later the figure had only risen to 1,330,783. According to Pamela Horn in *The Rise and Fall of the Victorian Servant*, this indicates a 'dramatic slowing down in the rate of expansion'. This slowing down continued up to the First World War, with just 1,359,359 female domestic servants recorded on the 1911 census.

Although the common perception of domestic servants is that of those working for the gentry in country houses, most servants did not work in such large households. In fact, in 1871, almost two-thirds of Britain's female domestic servants were classed as 'general servants' in one- or two-servant households.

However, the opposite was true for male servants as they were mostly found in households that kept large numbers of domestic staff. By the end of the nineteenth century, only the very wealthy retained their male staff. In *Keeping Their Place: Domestic Service in the Country House*, Pamela Sambrook argues that 'One of the major trends in domestic service throughout the nineteenth and twentieth centuries was the replacement of men by women, who were cheaper to employ and considered more biddable.'

With the exception of mining and manufacturing districts, the majority of jobs available for working-class girls in nineteenth-century Britain were in domestic service, especially in agricultural areas.

The situation was very different in industrial areas, particularly in northern towns with cotton and woollen factories and mills. Working in these places was considered more favourable than being a domestic servant, especially after the Factory Acts limited working hours. Once a girl had completed her hours, her leisure time was her own and she was not at the beck and call of her employer. In *My Ancestor Was in Service: A Guide to Sources for Family Historians*, Pamela Horn notes that 'to be a servant in industrial Lancashire was regarded by many working people as something to be ashamed of and as socially inferior to other kinds of occupation.' Shop work was now also attractive to girls who might once have only considered going into service for the same reasons.

Despite the general slowing down in the expansion of the number of servants, by the end of the nineteenth century, domestic service was still a significant employer. Miss Collet's *Report on the Money Wages of Indoor Domestic Servants* (1899) found that 'one third of the occupied female population of the UK are engaged in domestic service.'

The middle classes copied the ideas of the gentry regarding privacy and the segregation of staff, even in the most modest of homes without separate staircases or servants' quarters. Segregation was considered necessary to maintain the master–servant relationship, especially if the employer was not very far removed from the social class of his or her servant. To do this, for example, a maid of all work was often forced to eat, sleep and work by herself with very little social interaction between her and the employer.

An indication of the male domestic servant's place in society as a whole can be seen in the fact that they were excluded from enfranchisement under the 1884 Reform Act. As they were resident in their master's household, they were not themselves householders and could not satisfy the main franchise qualification. Outdoor servants who rented cottages from their employer were, however, classed as householders.

The various Education Acts passed from 1870 onwards had an impact on the age at which a child could start to work. In 1880, education was made compulsory for children up to the age of 10, and this was raised to 11 in 1893 and 12 in 1899. The school-leaving age was raised again to 14 under further legislation in 1918.

With better education came a wider view of the world, and also new job

Postcard inscribed 'Maggie, our maid 1916'. Maggie is dressed for war work. Author's collection

opportunities for the more intelligent girls in nursing, teaching and clerical work. For many of the less well educated, shops and factories still provided more attractive employment than domestic service.

The Twentieth Century

Although a number of servants' trade unions were founded during the late nineteenth and early twentieth centuries, according to Pamela Horn in *The Rise and Fall of the Victorian Servant*, they 'did not lead to any spectacular improvements in their conditions, but served rather as a barometer of discontent.' It was government legislation, not specifically aimed at domestic servants, which arguably created the greatest changes, namely the Old Age Pensions Act and the National Insurance Bill.

From 1 January 1909, people over the age of 70 could benefit from the first state pension introduced under the Old Age Pensions Act; this included domestic servants. If their income was less than eight shillings a week, they were entitled to a non-contributory pension of five shillings per week. There was a reduced pension for those with an income of between eight and twelve shillings per week, but anyone with a higher income than this received nothing. Applicants who had claimed poor relief in the previous two years were also excluded. For those ex-servants who were eligible, the new pension was a very welcome addition to their meagre incomes, and probably helped to keep them out of the workhouse.

The 1911 National Insurance Bill guaranteed manual workers sickness benefit and free medical treatment, and domestic servants were included in the legislation. Female servants were guaranteed 7s 6d for twenty-six weeks if they became ill, plus free medical treatment and a disablement benefit of 5s a week if they could not work after twenty-six weeks had passed. Both employer and female servant contributed 3d a week to the scheme. With the servant's contribution, the employer bought stamps to stick on the insurance card. Male servants paid a slightly higher contribution of 4d a week in return for a guaranteed 10s a week sickness benefit for twenty-six weeks.

There was great opposition to the Bill from many employers. According to Pamela Horn in *Life Below Stairs in the Twentieth Century*, they saw it as 'an intolerable interference by the state in domestic life and an insult to mistresses, implying that they neglected their servants when they were ill'. Nevertheless, the legislation was passed in 1911, coming into effect in July 1912, and the 'stamp' became part and parcel of domestic service.

The lot of domestic servants started to improve in the early years of the twentieth century, but despite a proliferation of labour-saving products and devices such as soap, polish and vacuum cleaners, uptake was very slow. It was still far cheaper to employ servants than it was to install gas in the house or baths with piped hot water. At this stage, as E S Turner points out in *What the Butler Saw: Two Hundred and Fifty Years of the Servant Problem*, 'the most important labour-saving device of all was still lacking: a sensibly designed house.'

While the winds of change had been blowing in the years up to the First World War, the conflict itself accelerated the transformation. It offered female servants the ultimate opportunity to leave domestic service for war work offering higher pay and more freedom. They worked in the munitions

Postcard of unidentified servants, 1930s. Author's collection

factories, as land girls, nurses and bus conductresses, and in shops and canteens. They were often employed in jobs previously carried out by skilled or semi-skilled men.

Male servants were expected to enlist, providing they were medically fit and were not over the maximum age. On the large country estates, most male servants left to fight for king and country – according to Pamela Horn, during the war an estimated 400,000 servants left domestic service for the armed forces and various areas of war production.

After the war, women who had worked in men's roles were expected to leave these posts, but having had a taste of independence, they were reluctant to go back to domestic service. Employers found it increasingly difficult to find and retain servants, and in the wealthier households living conditions were often improved to attract the right applicants.

In her memoir *Below Stairs*, Margaret Powell recalled her last place as cook in the 1920s before she married. It was in Montpelier Square, Knightsbridge and there she saw the change in the status of domestic servants: 'Here we really counted as part of the household . . . we each had a bedroom of our own . . . I was asked if there was anything I wanted changed, if I had enough clothes on the bed, if I wanted any more lights in the room . . .' On top of this, the kitchen was 'furnished with every appliance that was then known, and . . . it was light and airy. In the scullery the sink was white enamel, not one of those cement affairs, and aluminium saucepans, which was a change from either iron or copper. All our uniforms were provided free.'

Even in the years of high unemployment in the 1920s and 1930s, the move away from residential domestic service continued. A trend developed of servants becoming 'daily helps' or char-women, which meant they had fixed hours and were able to return home at the end of the day.

Chapter 2

PLACES OF WORK

There was a surprisingly wide range of places in which your servant ancestor could have worked, particularly in the nineteenth century when the middle classes started employing servants. At the top of the tree was the gentleman's country estate or its equivalent townhouse in London. A level below that were the homes of the professional classes such as doctors, lawyers and clergy, and then small middle-class households, followed by tradesmen and shopkeepers. Hotels, schools and hospitals were also employers of servants, while farms and lodging houses were at the bottom of the scale.

An engraving of Fountains Hall, Yorkshire from a drawing by William Richardson. Author's collection

Large Country Estates

In the servant world, true 'gentleman's service' involved working on a large country estate for the nobility, and gaining a place in such a household was considered the pinnacle of a servant's career.

The indoor staff was made up of those who worked above stairs and servants who stayed out of sight below stairs. Above stairs were the housekeeper, butler, under-butler, valet, footman, under-footman, lady's maid, parlourmaid, page or hall-boy, and, if there were children in the household, the nursery staff, comprising governess, head nurse, and nurse-maid. If the house was a very large one, there might also be a house steward.

Below stairs were the cook with her kitchen-maid, scullery maid and stillroom maid. There were also housemaids and perhaps a boot-boy. Laundry-maids and dairymaids also fell into this category.

A full complement of outdoor staff was also kept, which might include gardeners, gamekeepers, coachmen, grooms and stable-boys. In the early years of the twentieth century, the chauffeur began to replace the coachman. The lives of these outdoor staff were generally less restricted than their indoor counterparts since they were usually provided with accommodation on the estate. These roles were also better suited to male staff who wanted to marry and have a family.

In the servants' quarters, whether in a large country house or a small household, a strict social hierarchy was maintained at all times. Junior servants were expected to address their seniors with the deference accorded to their position. The butler was always 'Sir' and the housekeeper 'Madam'. The cook and housekeeper were referred to as 'Mrs' whether they were married or not, whereas the lady's maid and governess were always 'Miss'.

Servants in a large household or country house usually benefited from the camaraderie of the other staff and had support from each other. There was also a clear sub-division of roles. In his memoir *What the Butler Winked At: Being the Life and Adventures of Eric Horne, Butler*, Eric Horne recalled working as an under-butler to a noble family in 'the most regulated situation' he had ever been in. 'Everything went like clockwork, no confusion, no jealousies, no treading on each other's toes: no occasion for saying I didn't know this or that; for each department got their orders and acted up to them. Servants seldom wanted to leave that place unless they had been there some time and wanted promotion. I think what kept them together to a great extent was we were allowed a dance on the first Tuesday in every month.'

An entirely different class of servant was on the staff of the landed gentry than those who served the middle classes. A correspondent to the *Pall Mall Gazette* (24 May 1865) warned that 'There are as many classes of servants as there are classes of income, and it is generally unwise to engage a servant who has lived in an establishment of superior pretensions to one's own.'

The cost of maintaining a staff of servants was considerable, but they were indispensable in a large country house. Such a property simply could not be run without an army of servants, especially if the master and mistress were fond of entertaining.

Mrs Earle, the author of 'Eighteen Hundred A Year' in the *Cornhill Magazine* (July 1901) commented that '. . . every maid represents an additional £60 or £70 a year, and every man-servant another £70 or £80. These sums cover all expenses connected with a servant, including wages.'

For those with larger incomes and at least two properties, the costs of employing servants multiplied accordingly. In 'Ten Thousand A Year' in the *Cornhill Magazine* (August 1901), Lady Agnew estimated that 'The wages of twelve or fourteen servants would average between £350 and £400, and the upkeep of a London and a country house in linen, etc. would be close upon £200. There would then be £200 yearly for wine, £130 for coal, £70 for lighting, £130 for the butler's book which includes all telegrams, postage of letters and parcels, hampers, cabs, etc, £70 indoor liveries . . .'

Professional Classes

Men in professions such as doctors, lawyers and clergymen, or those in the civil service, earned around £800 per year. According to G Colmore writing in the *Cornhill Magazine* (June 1901), at this level of salary 'two is the right number [of servants], a cook at £20 a year, and house-parlourmaid at £18.' If the two servants were 'well-meaning and fairly intelligent', it was possible to have a household 'conducted with order and daintiness' but only if the mistress was willing to supervise the establishment and the master was his own butler. Colmore advised the mistress to dust the china and ornaments to prevent breakages and to give the servant more time to get through her morning's tasks. She also needed to be her own housekeeper, taking charge of her store and linen cupboards, inspecting every article after washing, and possibly assisting in the mending.

The view that only a small number of servants was actually needed in a household was backed up by Charles Booth in Volume 8 of his *Life and Labour of the People in London*. He argued that 'With three servants – a cook, parlourmaid and housemaid – a household is complete in all its functions; all else is only a development of this theme.'

In 1897, newly married Molly Hughes was living with her husband Arthur, a lawyer, in a flat in Ladbroke Grove, London, said to be six-roomed, with kitchen and bathroom. In *A London Home of the 1890s*, she recalled getting the bedroom ready for her first servant: 'I had a rooted idea that a servant's bedroom must have pink chintz covered with muslin round her table. With some trouble I had managed to buy these things beforehand, and now I had but to nail them on to a little table, make up her trestle bed and lay out her caps and aprons.'

Molly had no difficulty finding a servant as a friend had recommended 18-year-old Emma from East Dereham in Norfolk. 'I had made arrangements to meet her at the terminus on the following afternoon. I found Emma a fresh-faced, cheerful country girl. She sang, more or less all day long, odd snatches of hymns and popular songs.'

Emma was quickly found to be a 'treasure': 'She not only knew how to work, but knew what to work at – a still more valuable asset . . . I had vague ideas that servants were busy all the time, but what they were busy at was a mystery. Emma had a special day for "turning out" each room, always cleaned the silver on Friday, and devoted Saturday to the kitchen. As for washing, I wished she had kept a special day for that, but she had a penchant for washing, and would wash at all hours.'

'In a Servants' Hall: Servant London', Living London, 1902

Middle-Class Families

In *Early Victorian Britain 1832–1851*, J F C Harrison argues that 'servants were both indispensable to the middle class as a class, and at the same time were the Greatest Plague of Life.' The latter was the title of a comic volume by Henry and Augustus Mayhew published in 1847, subtitled: 'The adventures of a lady in search of a good servant'.

There was a proliferation of manuals published for the middle-class reader, for whom keeping servants was new. These included Mrs Beeton's *Book of Household Management* (1861), Mrs Florence Caddy's *Household Organisation* (1877), and Mrs J E Panton's *From Kitchen to Garret: Hints to Young Householders* (1888). They dealt with the duties of servants, household rules and etiquette when hiring staff.

However, such niceties were unnecessary for tradesmen, clerks and shopkeepers who fell into the category of the lower middle classes and could only afford one maid of all work. For the painter Ford Madox Brown, keeping a servant was very problematic, especially as his income was low. Extracts from his diary are published in *English Diaries of the Nineteenth Century*, edited by James Aitken, and in it he writes that he found a young girl through Barnet Union Workhouse, who was 'hard-working and reasonably good in her behaviour'. However, she 'seemed to be cursed with the devil's own temper, which made her uncontrollably surly at times, also at times insufferably insolent . . .'

On 26 August 1854, he wrote:

> Yesterday we were going into London, and she [the maid] was to take Katty for a walk while we were absent. On account of the cholera now everywhere, I cautioned her not to take the child into any house. She answered, 'I won't take the child out at all.' She stuck to this; I to the fact that servants must do what they are told, or leave. She was obstinate; I told her she should leave the house that minute . . . Before one she was gone. I gave her wages up to the day, and one month clear; so she went off with 12*s* 6*d*. Her wages were £5 a year, everything found her. If this is poor wages for a girl, I myself am very poor, and cannot help it. She had a good place in all except wages, but wanted sense to keep it. Where she is gone I know not.'

Unlike other employers who may not have given the business a second thought, the dismissal of his servant caused Ford Madox Brown a great deal of misery:

I feel like a scoundrel. Yet it was her own fault – I was not even cross with her to draw forth her insolence. I don't know what to think of it; I must endeavour to forbear passion in future and all haste. Had I not been angered, I might have found some way to adjust matters without proceeding to extremities . . .

For some middle-class households, keeping up appearances was everything, even if their income was too low to employ servants. As a cook in London in the 1920s, Margaret Powell worked for three months for a Jewish couple who had resorted to using temporary staff. In *Below Stairs*, she commented,

> The trouble was they couldn't afford to keep three maids, but the house was of a size that couldn't be run with less than three. Even as it was, nothing really got done as it should have been done. Everything looked old and shabby, except for her bedroom and the drawing-room . . . All the utensils were worn out . . . and nothing ever got replaced. I'm not surprised they advertised for temporary maids. They knew they wouldn't keep them for any time.

General servants were often employed by shopkeepers with small premises, usually single-handed, and often to take care of the cooking, cleaning and the children while the wife assisted in the shop. Like all positions where a servant was the only one in the household, hours were long and the work was difficult, especially if there was conflict between the shopkeeper and his wife about what the servant was expected to do.

Lodging Houses

Maids working in lodging houses were most definitely the Cinderellas of domestic servants. According to Jessie Boucherett's article 'Legislative Restrictions on Women's Labour' in *Englishwoman's Review* (1873), before about 1870, it was 'no uncommon thing for a lodging-house maid to be at work from six in the morning till eleven at night, getting no rest except at meal times, and even to have these short intervals broken into by the lodger's bell'.

Gradually, improvements were made as a result of the apparent 'scarcity' of servants caused by girls choosing shops and factories to work in rather than domestic service. This left maids in lodging houses with some bargaining power, and it became more common for them to be able to go to bed at 10 pm and to have an afternoon out every other Sunday.

As Jessie Boucherett pointed out, 'the scarcity [of servants] merely means that a healthy, honest, intelligent girl cannot now be compelled to work till her health breaks down for moderate wages.'

Farms

English and Welsh farm servants were traditionally hired at statute or 'mop' fairs held at Michaelmas (late September). They were usually engaged for a calendar year. The employment of Scottish farm servants was slightly different as they were hired at feeing markets, which were held twice a year at Whitsun (May) and Martinmas (November). They were therefore engaged for six months at a time. Across the country, the salaries of farm servants included accommodation and a food allowance. In Scotland in the 1860s many farms still operated the old system of boarding the servants in the kitchen. The more progressive farms provided bothys for their unmarried servants and cottages for married couples. By contrast, farm labourers were paid on a daily basis and did not live in.

The duties of female farm servants might include milking the cows and

Male farm servants at West Mains Farm, Duffus, 1919. From left to right: J McKay, Jimmy Phimister, Jock Crombie, Spence, Ewan Simpson ('bothy loon'), Barney Jenkins, W McKay, Colin Stewart. Courtesy of Falconer Museum, Forres

collecting eggs, as well as helping in the farmhouse. One girl who started in service on a farm was Margaret (Maggie) Welch whose story is told in M C Scott-Moncrieff's *Yes, Ma'am! Glimpses of Domestic Service 1901–1951*. Born in the late nineteenth century, Maggie was a coal-miner's daughter from Lanarkshire and went into service at the age of fourteen:

> I went to the feeing-market in Glasgow where I was hired by a farmer to take care of his four children whose ages ranged from eleven years to four months, the wages to be £9 a year in two instalments, and a day off to take it home. It was a very unhappy period in my life. Rising at 4.30am, my first task was to cook a large pot of porridge to breakfast nine people including myself. One morning I left the stirring to attend Baby who woke crying. The farmer's words when hiring me Baby was to be my first charge. That's why the porridge got burnt. The farmer's wife . . . took a stick from the wall and wrapped me hard over the knuckles. Many a time I got struck with it . . . In the year at the farm I learned the dreadful pangs of homesickness. I worked out my year . . . I was fond of the children and very sad to part from them.

Hotels

Another area in which servants could work was 'public service' in a hotel in one of the cities or tourist resorts. Here, all kinds of servants were employed, from chambermaids and bell-boys through to kitchen staff and waiters. Although hotels did not always have a good reputation, it appears that working in 'public service' rather than 'private service' for a family allowed for far greater freedom and time off, and salaries could be supplemented with substantial tips.

There are a number of letters from servants in *Toilers in London; or Inquiries Concerning Female Labour in the Metropolis* (Anon, 1889) on Lee Jackson's Victorian London website (www.victorianlondon.org). One is from 'A Contented Chambermaid', who extolled the virtues of working in public service. She was employed in a 'select' hotel where she had thirteen rooms to look after, and had been there for five years. Her salary was £17 per annum and in the previous year, she had been able to make it up to £25 through tips.

She added:

> . . . we are fifteen chambermaids, and we do the rooms between us. All our work is done by three in the afternoon, and then we dress,

and we have tea at five, after which we light up, and then we've nothing to do but to mind our bells till we do the rooms at eight o'clock. We go to bed at ten . . . Our food is beautiful because we have the leavings from the table . . . We have great fun among us servants . . . I know the public service has a bad name, but that is because some hotels keep fast girls to bring gentlemen about the place, and in a select hotel like ours the housekeeper would send us away if we were flighty. The housekeeper is very strict, but she don't interfere when us leave work at three o'clock, and she gives us our days out as it comes convenient.

Maggie Welch's third position was on the fourth floor of Glasgow's Central Hotel. She recalled: 'That's where you see life – in a big hotel.' Her post was as bell-maid with a limited amount of cleaning, two hours off each day and all her Friday afternoons free. While on duty she sat and waited in a little room, ready to answer bells from the bedrooms and act accordingly. She 'thoroughly enjoyed life on the fourth floor, and shared the fun with the other maids.'

At the end of the season, the floor manager auctioned the miscellaneous unclaimed objects left in the bedrooms. Maggie acquired for twopence a smart blue velour hat and an empty suitcase nobody wanted. She next found a seasonal job waitressing at a restaurant in St Andrews through the registry office in Sauchiehall Street, Glasgow, and met her future husband there.

Institutions: Schools/Hospitals

In any institution where large numbers of people were accommodated, servants were vital to ensure the smooth running of the place. Cooking, cleaning and bed-changing were all undertaken by servants and the work was hard and relentless. This was especially true if the servants were expected to live in because they were then bound by the rules of the institution like the other staff. Unlike hotels with paying guests, there was also no prospect of supplementing meagre salaries with tips. Working in a large institution did not therefore offer the best working conditions, unless perhaps work was found in a small private school, for example.

The exception was in hospitals. Before a system of training for hospital nurses was put into place in the 1870s, the usual route into nursing was for potential recruits to start as 'scrubbers', work their way up to ward-maids and from there, on to become a nurse. Scrubbers and ward-maids therefore had the opportunity to 'better themselves' as nurses, and improve their pay.

The Servant Problem

The servant problem – the apparent inability of employers to obtain and keep good servants – seems to have been much in evidence during the second half of the nineteenth century and into the twentieth. There were countless opinions offered on both sides as to the cause, and the remedy, including that given by Mrs Panton in *From Kitchen to Garret*. Mrs Panton was Jane Ellen Panton, daughter of the painter William Powell Frith. In her manual, she was proud to state that: 'I have had twenty years' experience of household management. I have had three cooks in the time, and have never had a maid give me "warning"...'

Her advice would seem to be common sense, but it was contrary to the way in which many mistresses viewed their servants: 'If we treat our maids just as we treat ourselves we shall find our trouble almost disappear. I invariably leave my maids a good deal to themselves about their work; and once they know what has to be done, I find it is done without my constantly being after them ...'

Mrs Panton stressed the need to build a good relationship with servants: 'We may accept it as an axiom that we cannot have nice, good servants unless we take the trouble of either training them ourselves, or get them from a mistress who has had an eye over the well-being of her maidens ...'

She concluded that 'To have good and loving servants ... it is necessary to have them tolerably young, to be firm, kind, and, above all, sympathetic, to know as much about their home life as is possible ... sympathy is the bond that should unite mistress and maid ... Never be afraid to praise your servants ... they are far more likely to remain where they are appreciated and cared for than where they know they are only looked upon as so much necessary furniture ...'

In 1878, 'A Housekeeper' wrote to the *Manchester Weekly Times* about the so-called domestic-servant difficulty:

> I live in the fashionable suburb of a large manufacturing town, and I have constant complaints from nearly all my friends of their difficulty in getting good servants, and in some cases getting servants at all ... In my own house, where the work is heavy, and three servants do it all, I have one nine years, one eight and one nearly seven, and yet I maintain that these servants are not exceptional, but merely fair types of the class. The question is often put to me, 'How do you manage to keep your servants?' The answer is by being kind to them,

showing them a human sympathy and interest, and trusting them whenever I can.

'A Housekeeper' was adamant that 'the habit of continual faultfinding does infinite harm'. She added:

> . . . scold as little as possible, and when you do, let it be about something of grave importance, some point affecting the moral atmosphere of your household; and then be as severe as you please . . . Then in the matter of trusting your servants . . . it is my experience that with open cupboards (except, of course, wine and spirits) advantage will seldom be taken by the servants. Let us not look upon servants as our natural enemies, or they will speedily justify the appellation.

It was not necessarily the work itself which servants found degrading; above all, they resented their loss of freedom. For most servants, according to Trevor May in *The Victorian Domestic Servant*, 'the bitterest pill to take was the necessity of adopting a servile attitude towards their employers.'

Chapter 3

WHO WENT INTO SERVICE?

Unless they lived in a mining or manufacturing district that offered alternative employment, working-class girls usually went into service at about the age of 12 or 13, or sometimes earlier if their parents needed them to contribute to the family's income. By 1899, the compulsory school-leaving age was 12.

Within this group of girls were those who were sent into service from workhouses or poorhouses, and charitable institutions such as Dr Barnardo's. Children of parents already working on a landed estate also naturally went into service. The final group were widows or married women in reduced circumstances, most of whom had been in service before marriage and returned to the work.

Children of the Working Classes

Going into service for the first time must have been a nerve-wracking and, at times, terrifying experience. In many cases, girls had to leave their villages and all they knew to find work in towns. They took with them their scanty belongings in servants' boxes, probably the same ones their mothers had used before them.

The best place for someone going into service for the first time was one in which there were other servants in the household – they could act as mentors, showing the ropes and explaining the various foibles of the employers so that he or she knew what to expect. However, this was not always possible and many found themselves as maids of all work thrown in at the deep end, and quite alone.

For some, the first experience of domestic service was positively traumatic. Mrs Wrigley, a plate layer's wife, was born in Cefn Mawr, Wales in 1858. In *Life As We Have Known It, By Co-operative Working Women*, edited by Margaret Llewelyn Davies, she recalled how she worked in service before her marriage. She was sent to her first proper place at the tender age of 9: 'The doctor's wife came to our house and said a lady and gentleman wanted a little nurse for their child to go back with them to Hazel Grove, near

Stockport. My little bundle of clothes was packed up and I went in full glee with them.'

Mrs Wrigley's joy was short-lived. 'Instead of being a nurse I had to be a servant-of-all-work, having to get up at six in the morning, turn a room out and get it ready for breakfast. My biggest trouble was I could not light the fire, and my master was very cross and would tell me to stand away, and give me a good box on my ears.'

Being away from home made the experience even harder: 'I fretted very much for my home. Humble as it was, it was home. Not able to read or write, I could not let my parents know, until a kind old lady in the village wrote to my parents to fetch me home from the hardships I endured. I had no wages at this place, only a few clothes.'

Homesickness was a real problem for those new to domestic service and far from home. In 1915, a young male servant identified only as 'Bert' wrote a postcard to one of his married sisters in Dudley, Worcestershire from Cann Hall near Bridgnorth in Shropshire. It is not clear what role he was working in, but he was probably a boot- or hall-boy. He commented that, 'It is rather lonely here without brothers & sisters,' and added, 'I envy you your class on Wednesday night', an indication of the frustration felt by domestic servants about their lack of freedom.

An unidentified female farm servant in Morayshire, circa 1910. Courtesy of Falconer Museum, Forres

In rural areas where there were few alternatives to domestic service, the daughters of women who had been servants would inevitably follow them into the same occupation. Born in 1844 in Gorsey Bank near Sheriffhales, Staffordshire, Jane Chetter was the daughter of an agricultural labourer. She went into service and was not at home with her parents on the 1861 census, but in October 1862 Jane had her first child Martha baptised. Martha was the first of five illegitimate daughters Jane was to have before her marriage. Agnes Mary was born in 1864, followed by Elizabeth in 1868. These first three children were born in Shifnal Union Workhouse but only Agnes Mary survived infancy.

Jane's pregnancies and children do not appear to have stopped her finding work in service, presumably because her parents were looking after Agnes Mary. By the time of the 1871 census, Jane was working on a farm as a general servant for the Walker family in Lilleshall, Shropshire. Her master, Henry Walker, farmed 251 acres and employed four men and four boys. Jane was the only servant in the household.

Two more illegitimate daughters were born to Jane: Sarah Ann in 1873 and Emily in 1877. Both survived infancy and in April 1879, Jane married Charles Powell, an agricultural labourer who was ten years her junior.

In due course, Jane's three illegitimate daughters all went into domestic service. In 1881, Agnes Mary was working as a cook in York for Charles and Frederica Ralph. The Ralphs had eleven children at home and Charles Ralph was a retired colonel, now an assistant commissary general for HM Ordnance. Despite this impressive title, it does not appear that the Ralphs had a very large income since, in addition to Agnes, there was only one housemaid and a nurse employed in the household. Without a kitchen-maid to help her, Agnes would have had a difficult job to cook for such a large family every day. She married John Emms, an engine driver, five years later.

In 1891, Agnes's sister, Sarah Ann, was working as a general servant in West Bromwich for James Tipler, a widowed grocer with two daughters aged 14 and 9. As the only servant in the household, Sarah Ann's workload would have been heavy, although the eldest daughter may have helped with some of the cooking and cleaning. Sarah Ann was recorded with her step-father's surname and four years later, she married Benjamin Tuckey, an ironworks stock-taker and part-time fireman.

Emily Chetter, the youngest of Jane's illegitimate daughters, moved to Manchester where she was working as a general servant in 1901 for William Eckersley, a fruit and potato dealer. She was the only servant employed there. William Eckersley's wife and eldest son were recorded as his assistants but

Alice White, Domestic Servant

Born in 1873 in Powick, Worcestershire, Alice Jane White was the youngest child of John and Phoebe White, who had nine other children. John was a farm labourer and on later censuses Phoebe was listed as a laundress. Alice had four sisters, three of whom went into domestic service before her.

In 1891 Alice was working as a domestic servant for Reverend Cecil Hughes, the rector of Powick, at the vicarage. In addition to the rector and his wife, there were four children in the family, aged 17, 9, 7 and 4. There was one other servant: 22-year-old Mary Cubberley, also from Powick, but their roles were not differentiated on the census.

However, a clue to Alice's role can be found in a studio photograph, in which she is dressed in a parlour maid's uniform with cap and apron. The photograph is inscribed 'Alice

Carte de visite of a servant inscribed 'Alice White, 1 October 1892'.
Author's collection

White, 1 October 1892'. Alice cannot be found on the 1901 census under her maiden name so it is likely she had married by this time.

there were also two young daughters in the household, aged 11 and 9. It is therefore likely that Emily's work was confined to the house and to looking after the children, rather than helping in the shop. Like her sister Sarah Ann, she was recorded as Powell, which was her step-father's surname. Emily married George Henry Webb five years later. (With thanks to Carl Higgs for this information about his ancestors.)

Children in Poor Law Institutions

While working-class girls formed the majority of those who went into service, within that group were female workhouse inmates who were found situations by the workhouse master or the guardians of the poor law union in which they lived. Many of these girls were orphans and if a situation did not work out, for whatever reason, they had no choice but to return to the workhouse. In Scotland, these institutions were known as poorhouses.

Letitia Husband was one such orphan. Born in 1863 in Sedgley, Staffordshire, she was admitted to the Dudley Union Workhouse with her brother John in November 1872. She was only 11 when she was first sent into service on 1 August 1874. It is not known how long this situation lasted, but she was sent to another place on 9 June 1875.

In September 1879, described as a 'destitute' servant, she was readmitted to the Dudley Union Workhouse, and the following year she entered the workhouse again on several occasions, each time discharging herself at her 'own desire'. As she was now an adult, by this time she would have been expected to find her own employment.

At the time of the 1881 census, 18-year-old Letitia was working as a general servant in Greenwich, London in the household of a retired provision merchant. There was one other general servant there too. However, by November of that year, Letitia was readmitted to Dudley Union Workhouse after being 'removed from Liverpool'. She was again sent into service on 6 December 1881 but was readmitted on 4 February 1882 as a destitute servant.

The entries relating to Letitia in the Dudley Union Workhouse Register of Admissions and Discharges recur regularly, with her being admitted as destitute and discharging herself, until 21 September 1882 when she was taken to the police station. This would only have happened if she had used threatening or violent behaviour towards the staff or other inmates, or she had repeatedly broken the rules of the workhouse. (G/DU 6/1/4-8, Dudley Archives and Local History Service)

At some point Letitia found her way to Leeds as it was there in May 1888 that she married William Parrington, a hawker. By 1901, the couple had moved to Barrow-in-Furness, Lancashire where William was a fish hawker. They had six children.

The stigma attached to anyone who had been a workhouse inmate made it difficult to find good places for young servants. Wealthy employers would not consider them, and the lower middle-class households or shops to which they were normally sent viewed them with suspicion. However, in 1911 the authors of *Cassell's Household Guide* commented that 'A girl from the workhouse . . . may be rough material, but she is often so willing, and so grateful for small kindnesses, that it is well worth while taking her in hand.'

It could be argued that workhouse girls were in a better position to start in service than those sent from their family homes since they had been given some form of training. From around the mid-nineteenth century, London poor law unions set up district schools separate from their workhouses where child inmates were sent. They underwent industrial training – for girls, this meant training for domestic service.

In 1850, Charles Dickens visited the pauper school at Norwood where there were 900 children. In his article 'London Pauper Children', published in *Household Words*, he wrote that the girls had 'three days' schooling and three days' training in household occupations – such as cleaning the house, washing, ironing, mangling and needlework'. When Dickens visited another industrial school at Swinton, near Manchester, he called it a 'pauper palace' because it was so well run.

Elizabeth Cook, 15 years old at the time, was sent into service from the City of London workhouse on 12 December 1879. The City of London Union Register of Children in Service or on Trial as Apprentices, 1874 – held at London Metropolitan Archives (and also available online through Ancestry: www.ancestry.co.uk) – records that she went to work as a general servant in the household of Thomas Laurence, a bank cashier, and his wife Anna. They lived at Hastings Cottage, Grange Park, Ealing and had one young child.

On 12 November 1880, Elizabeth was summarily sent back to the workhouse. The admission register records that she was 'Returned from service by reason of not getting up in the morning when called & ceasing to try & please her Mistress'. This suggests that, at first, Elizabeth was a good servant but that her efforts diminished. This may have had something to do with the fact that at the time of her dismissal the Laurences had a three-month-old baby who would probably have added to her workload. By 1881, they were employing a nurse-maid as well as a general servant, but it is not known if a similar servant was in place at the same time as Elizabeth, although this would have been usual.

Elizabeth's second situation in a lower middle-class household in Rosendale Road, West Dulwich lasted just six months, ending in June 1881. Here, she was employed by a stationer's warehouseman and his wife who had two young daughters, and, unlike her first situation, Elizabeth was the only servant. The final situation recorded for her in the City of London workhouse registers was with a Miss Marsh in Calthorp Street, off Russell Square. Elizabeth does not appear in the registers again.

A comic postcard dated 1909 with the caption 'Why she didn't get the place. The man behind the paper ventured the opinion that she might do'. Author's collection

It was in the interests of all poor law unions to provide good industrial training for its child inmates to reduce the chance of them returning to the workhouse. Despite this, poor law unions in the rest of the country were slow to follow London's example. However, by the 1870s and 1880s, most had started to address the issue.

Some unions chose to set up district schools away from the workhouse. The Wigmore schools, opened in 1872, were made up of children from the Walsall and West Bromwich unions. According to Frederick William Hackwood in *A History of West Bromwich,* industrial training was a vital part of the children's schooling at Wigmore and the boys were taught 'the trades of the tailor, shoemaker, baker, and gardener . . . the girls are employed in the laundry and at other useful domestic avocations'.

Other poor law unions worked with charitable organisations to better prepare their workhouse girls for the world of work. In the 1880s, the Dudley Union attempted to solve this problem. A 'training home' for some of the girls was established under the auspices of the Dudley Girls' Friendly Society 'for the purpose of training such girls for Domestic duties and obtaining for them suitable places of service'.

Workhouse girls were sent into domestic service between the ages of 11 and 13. Some workhouses advertised in the local newspaper for placements whilst others were approached directly by employers looking for servants. At smaller poor law unions, such as Sedgefield in County Durham, the master himself used his local contacts to find placements for the workhouse children.

Children sent from the workhouse into service were particularly vulnerable to exploitation by employers, since they often had no family to turn to if problems arose. A number of different charitable organisations sprang up to offer support, including the Metropolitan Association for Befriending Young Servants (MABYS), which concentrated on London, and the Girls' Friendly Society (GFS), which had branches all over the country.

The Metropolitan Association for Befriending Young Servants was founded in 1875 by Mrs Jane Nassau Senior, Britain's first female civil servant, and Henrietta Barnett, a social reformer. It aimed to provide support to girls discharged from London institutions such as workhouses and industrial schools and to steer them away from prostitution and alcoholism. It was the job of MABYS volunteers to visit the girls in their situations, something which did not always go down well with their mistresses. By the 1880s, the association had twenty-five branch offices and seventeen associated care homes. According to an article in *English Illustrated Magazine* (June 1894), in 1891 MABYS was keeping 'a benevolent oversight' of between 8,000 and 9,000 girls.

Born in 1888, Lilian Taylor was an inmate at Kensington Union Schools (Banstead) who was monitored by MABYS after being discharged from the workhouse in September 1902 and sent into service for a Mrs Mason of Gerrard's Lodge, Banstead. Reports about her progress appear in the Kensington Union Schools (Banstead) Report of Girls under the Care of the Metropolitan Association for Befriending Young Servants, 1904–1910, held in London Metropolitan Archives (also available online through Ancestry: www.ancestry.co.uk).

In 1904, Lilian was described as 'fairly satisfactory' and 'Doing fairly well in her 4th place, inclined to be rude, can work well when she wants to. 117 The Avenue, S. Ealing.' By 1905, her progress was deemed 'satisfactory'. Her report read: 'A good girl but far from strong. Just recovering from a severe attack of gastric ulcers & has been sent by MABYS to Eastbourne for rest & change. Her place is being kept open for her.' The fact that Lilian was not going to lose her place while spending time convalescing was a luxury that few sick servants ever had. The following year, she was described as 'Doing well as Housemaid in her present place, & is in much better health'.

In 1907 things were not going so well for Lilian: 'A nice pleasant girl but is not strong and has had to leave her place and go to a Convalescent Home. Her mistress gives her an excellent character.' However, a year later, Lilian's report read: 'Is in much better health; a good steady girl & her mistress is very satisfied with her. Now over age.' It is not known what happened to Lilian after this.

If a girl's report was unsatisfactory, she was sent to one of the MABYS training homes for further instruction. Certificates were awarded to members who had remained in service in one place for a specified period of time.

The Girls' Friendly Society (GFS) was founded in 1875 by Mrs Mary Elizabeth Townsend in association with the Church of England. Its main aim was to preserve the chastity of working-class girls and prevent them from falling into prostitution, especially those who had moved from the countryside into the towns to find work. It was intended that 'lady' associates would befriend and guide these girls who would become members of the society, and that the associates would form branches and give regular meetings for the members. Clergymen's wives were often associates. To become a member, girls had to be virtuous and remain a virgin until marriage. They could join the GFS from the age of 12, but from 1882 younger girls from 8 upwards could become candidates preparing to become members.

The society provided cheap accommodation in lodges to servants in-between posts, and 'homes of rest', which were similar to convalescent homes. By the end of 1875, there were twenty-five branches and between 2,000 and 3,000 members. Five years later, the Girls' Friendly Society had almost 40,000 members and more than 13,500 associates.

To aid servants further, the society set up its own registry offices and issued publications featuring advertisements for situations vacant and situations wanted. According to Vivienne Richmond, in 1897 the Girls' Friendly Society 'co-ordinated the formation of the Associated Guild of Registries, which compiled a "white list" of respectable registry offices.' Domestic servants were the largest single occupational group of the society membership.

The Girls' Friendly Society wanted to encourage its members to stay in their positions for longer periods of time. At first, they offered premiums of around five shillings a year to those who remained with their employer; this was later changed to a certificate commemorating 'Faithful Discharge of Duties'.

There were also plenty of smaller local charitable organisations which aimed to help and support servants to find work and to stay in employment. One example was the Manchester Society for the Improvement and Encouragement of Female Servants, established in 1816, which operated a registry office for servants. Its rules stated that 'Any female servant may have her name inserted who can give two respectable references for character.' Subscribers of one guinea or more became members of the society and for each guinea subscribed they could nominate one servant for the 'rewards and bestowments'.

If a servant had lived for two years with the same subscriber 'and attended public worship as regularly as her situation has permitted', and her employer certified her good conduct, she would receive £1 1s. This was increased to £1 11s after three years, and £2 2s after four years.

In addition, the rules stated that 'Any servant who has received two pecuniary rewards from this society, and shall at a future period of life become incapacitate, or have a large family, and indigent, may be annually assisted, at the discretion of the committee, with a gratuity not exceeding two guineas'. (DDPR 37/17, Lancashire Archives)

Children in Charitable Institutions

Charitable institutions also sent their inmates into service when they were old enough; the Foundling Hospital and Dr Barnardo's are two good examples.

Founded in 1741 by Thomas Coram, the Foundling Hospital in London was a children's home for the 'education and maintenance of exposed and deserted young children'. The children were illegitimate and were usually placed in the hospital's care by their mothers who, until the end of the eighteenth century, left an identifying token with the child to be used if they wanted to claim him or her at a later date. The Foundling Hospital carefully vetted potential employers and, according to Pamela Horn in *My Ancestor was in Service*, 'successful masters and mistresses had to be housekeepers, of the Protestant religion, must not let lodgings and, in the case of a male employer, they had to be married.'

Dr Thomas John Barnardo founded his first home for destitute boys in 1870, and later opened the Girls' Village Home in Barkingside, housing 1,500 girls. Barnardo's boys and girls were taught skills to enable them to earn a living when they left. In the case of girls, this meant training in domestic work, which was taught at the Barkingside Home.

Charity schools also had requests from employers for domestic servants, and their registers often record instances of girls being sent into service. Among their lessons, the pupils of Lancaster Girls' Charity School were taught cleaning and sewing. They left when they reached the age of 14, either for domestic service or to work in one of the nearby mills.

On 13 January 1877, an entry in the ledger recorded that a share of the money was distributed to the girls '. . . as a reward for cleaning the last half year, also gave to those girls who have been admitted last year each a cloak'.

Annie Gregson was one of the school's pupils, and she was called out for employment on 1 May 1876, 'having turned 14 years of age'. By 10 August, she was 'present for lessons again after three weeks Domestic Employment'. Annie was sent out to work at regular intervals and on 26 March 1877, she 'received as a reward for general good conduct, a Holy Bible, Church prayer book & servant's book'. (SMQ 6/1, Lancashire Archives)

By 1881, Annie Gregson was working as a kitchen-maid for an architect in Scotsforth, Lancashire, who had a wife and three grown-up children. There were three other servants on the staff: a cook, a housemaid and a waitress.

Another organisation, the Female Aid Society, was highlighted by *Punch* (3 March 1866) as a 'well-directed charity' providing a 'Home for Friendless Young Females'. It commented:

> People who are always complaining of bad servants should subscribe to this Society, whose aim is to make good ones. The complaint is now almost as universal as the cattle-plague: and were each of the complainants every year to send a sovereign to the Female Aid Society (27, Red Lion Square), we should not hear so much talk of the willfulness of housemaids and the wastefulness of cooks.

Children of Estate Workers

The landed gentry had a regular supply of new servants as the offspring of their estate workers usually went into service at the 'big house'. Robert Waller, the groom and later coachman at Eden Hall, Cumbria lived with his wife Elizabeth on the Eden Hall estate. They had four children, three of whom went into domestic service, and two found employment at Eden Hall itself.

The oldest child, Martha Ann Waller was born in 1844. Unusually, she was still listed as a scholar aged 17 on the 1851 census and was living at home. She cannot be found on the 1861 or 1871 censuses, but by 1881 she

Postcard of unidentified outdoor staff with barrow, circa 1900. Author's collection

was working as a housemaid at Fenton House, Nesbit, Northumberland. She was still there in 1891 and 1901. In 1891, it was the home of 67-year-old Henry J Morton (who was living on his own means) and his two sisters, one unmarried, one widowed.

A large number of servants were kept in addition to Martha: a housekeeper, a cook, a laundry-maid, a kitchen-maid, another housemaid, two lady's maids, a poultry woman, two footmen plus a coachman living at Fenton Lodge. By 1901, the staff was reduced to just Martha and one other general servant, although the rest of the household may have been elsewhere as the census was taken at the start of the London season – this was the period between April and August when the gentry moved from their country houses to the capital for five months of socialising.

John Waller, born in 1845, was recorded as a helper at Eden Hall on the 1861 census, which probably meant he was a boot- or hall-boy. He followed in his father's footsteps by becoming a coachman at Eden Hall, where he was listed on the 1871 census. He cannot be found on the 1881 or 1891 censuses, but by 1901 he was a widower and had left domestic service. He was working as a railway timekeeper in Carlisle and had a housekeeper in his household.

Eliza Jane Waller, the youngest child, born in 1849, became the lady's maid at Eden Hall from at least 1868, when she signed a wages receipt for £9 for half a year. She was still listed as working at Eden Hall on the 1871 census, but by 1881 she was living with her parents in Edenhall village as 'lady's maid, domestic servant unemployed'.

Widows or Married Women in Reduced Circumstances

It was not just children who went into service. Widows or married women who had fallen on hard times often returned to service to make ends meet. If this meant living in with the family, any children they had ended up being looked after by relatives, and siblings were often scattered between homes.

Even unmarried women, who had not previously worked but needed to earn money simply because of the misfortunes life dealt them, might try to obtain a position as a governess, housekeeper or lady's companion.

H G Wells's mother, Sarah (née Neal) worked at Uppark as a housekeeper from 1880 to 1893. She had first been in service there as a lady's maid in 1850 before marrying three years later. Her husband Joseph had been a gardener at Uppark and had taken on a china shop in the High Street in Bromley, Kent. He was also a professional cricketer, but in 1877 he fractured his thigh and his cricketing career was over. As a lower middle-class shopkeeper, Joseph struggled to earn enough to provide for Sarah and his four children.

In *Late Victorian Britain 1875–1901*, J F C Harrison quotes from H G Wells's memoirs: 'The only domestic help I ever knew [my mother] to have was a garrulous old woman of the quality of Sairey Gamp, a certain Betsy Finch. In opulent times Betsy would come in to char . . .'

Times were tough and Sarah Wells was ashamed of the situation she was in, but appearances still had to be kept up at all costs. 'She believed that it was a secret to all the world that she had no servant and did all the household drudgery herself. I was enjoined never to ask questions about it or let it out when I went abroad.'

At the age of 58, Sarah was forced to return to domestic service for the same mistress at Uppark. According to Pamela Sambrook in *Keeping Their Place*, by 1892 at the age of 70, she was 'a pathetic figure, increasingly deaf and easily irritated, far from an efficient housekeeper, given to gossiping and passing on imaginary tales to her mistress'. She was given a month's notice in January 1893, but by this time, her son H G Wells 'was already in the process of establishing himself as a writer and could afford to arrange a home for her.' She died in 1905.

Chapter 4

FINDING WORK

How did your ancestor find work as a domestic servant? This would depend on where he or she lived or wanted to work, but there were four main ways in which to find a place. Responding to an employer's newspaper advertisement or being personally recommended for a position were popular means of finding work. Statute or hiring fairs were common in market towns until the mid-nineteenth century, while servants' registry offices provided an alternative way to find employment in domestic service.

Hiring Fairs

It was traditional for all farm servants to attend 'statute' or 'hiring' fairs (also sometimes called 'mop' fairs) to find employment. In England and Wales, they were held annually, usually at Michaelmas. However, in Scotland, they were known as feeing markets and were held twice a year at Whitsun and Martinmas. They stood in the marketplace, holding emblems of their occupations, waiting to be picked out by a local farmer or squire. Female servants who attended the fairs were usually dairymaids, but cooks and housemaids might also be found there holding a basting spoon and broom respectively. The cook wore red ribbons, while a housemaid wore white.

If satisfactory answers were given to questions asked, the employer would give each servant a shilling in proof of the hiring, leaving them free for the rest of the day. Once engaged, the farm servant bought streamers of red, white and blue ribbon, which he pinned in his hat to show he had a new master, and then enjoyed the shows, roundabouts, and all the fun of the fair.

It was this last part of the fair which drew the most criticism, with accusations that the fairs encouraged drunkenness and unruly behaviour. By the mid-nineteenth century, the ancient custom of hiring fairs was dying out, although in 1888 *The Graphic* commented that 'there are still a few sleepy, out of the way market-towns and cities where they yet linger, with most of

'An English Statute Fair', The Graphic, *10 March 1888*

their ancient rights and observances.' According to Trevor May in *The Victorian Domestic Servant*, the fairs 'remained significant in some areas including Wales, the south of Scotland and the north of England, and had not disappeared before 1914.'

Personal Recommendation

When a servant needed a new place, personal recommendation was a useful way of finding one. The landed gentry, particularly in the eighteenth and early nineteenth centuries, were accustomed to calling upon their network of friends, acquaintances and business colleagues when they required new servants. Estate records across the country include countless examples of correspondence recommending servants for friends, usually between females. In most cases, recommendations for servants came from other genteel women.

However, as Amanda Vickery points out in *The Gentlemen's Daughter: Women's Lives in Georgian England*, tradeswomen also provided important contacts and 'shopkeepers, mantua-makers and milliners are revealed as important intermediaries between two worlds of women.' She adds that, of the numerous tasks the mistress of a genteel household had to deal with, 'by far the most tedious was the acquisition and retention of honest, loyal and efficient servants'. Gentlewomen spent a great deal of time and effort in pursuing new servants, and in trying to keep them.

While most correspondence in search of servants comes from the mistress of the house, widowers often had to undertake this task themselves. One such letter can be found in the Matthew Boulton archive which Shena Mason quotes from in *The Hardware Man's Daughter: Matthew Boulton and his 'Dear Girl'*. Having remodelled Soho House, Birmingham in the 1790s as his main residence, industrialist Matthew Boulton needed servants he could trust and rely on. His wife had died in 1783, leaving his daughter Anne as the mistress of the house.

In 1795, Charlotte Matthews, the wife of Boulton & Watt's banker in London, wrote to Boulton with details of a replacement housekeeper. Speaking generally of the servant situation at Soho, Boulton replied:

> I am determind to avoid takeing any of the subordinate Maids from Birmgm as their Relations & connections are sure to crowd my House on Sunday & when I am absent. I therefore prefer Lincolnshire or any shire to this Neighbourhood. Dosey is a very good cook & Kitty, tho ugley, a good Chambermaid and Taberner a trifling foolish body, that is more likely to please a Master than a Mistress, but they are constantly quarrelling with each other & rude to my Daughter. I am therefore determind to have a new sett for I will have peace in Israel. (MS 3782/12/68/154, MB-Charlotte Matthews, 24 Nov 1795, Birmingham Archives and Heritage Service)

In her *Book of Household Management,* Isabella Beeton acknowledged that there were some respectable registry offices, but she recommended 'the mistress to make inquiry amongst her circle of friends and acquaintances, and her tradespeople. The latter generally know those in their neighbourhood, who are wanting situations . . .'

Lower down the social scale, the local vicar's wife might recommend a girl for her first place in a middle-class household or a current employer might put her own servant forward for a position which would be a step up for him or her.

The Galton family of Warwickshire seem to have been particularly active in finding servants for their friends and family. In this letter from Mary Galton to her brother-in-law John Howard Galton, she writes about the difficulties of finding a housekeeper for John. He had married Isabella Strutt the previous year and they were to settle at Hadzor House, Droitwich:

17 January 1820

My dear Howard,

I have been busily employed lately in writing and reading about Housekeepers; [Miss Patterson] sent me the particulars of what Isabella would require, and by today's post I have sent it to London. I have heard of seven good ones, two of them very good, and Mrs Norman has sent two others to Susan to see, but they would neither of them answer for us being too much accustomed to London and not understanding country things, viz. hams, bacon, preserves, & all of which are bought in Town. One I have heard of today I think very likely to suit . . . she has studied under two Man Cooks in Noblemens families and perfectly understands foreign cooking . . . (MS 3101/C/D/10/7/4, Birmingham Archives and Heritage Service)

In an undated letter, John Howard Galton's brother Hubert also recommended a footman to him:

A Footman will call on you at Dudson on Monday evening, he is Nephew to Everett the Stationers in Cherry Steeple, 26 years of age wants 35 Guineas which is to include two Liveries or he will wear his own clothes, he has lived two years and a half with a Mr Freeman of Radway by Edgehill who gives him an excellent character except in one particular, viz, that he was too fond of the ladies which was the occasion of his parting with him. You will decide on Monday whether he will suit you or not – for my own part I should like an older person. (MS 3101/C/D/10/7/6, Birmingham Archives and Heritage Service)

Newspaper Advertisements

Perusing the 'Situations Vacant' columns in the local newspaper was often the first port of call when searching for a new place. If a servant had been unable to find a suitable position in this way, and did not want to use a registry office, he or she might place an advertisement themselves in the 'Situations Wanted' column. This was less common as it cost money to do so, but according to Pamela Horn in *Life Below Stairs in the Twentieth Century*,

REQUIRED, for a gentleman's family, in the country, a highly respectable person, as thorough COOK. Kitchenmaid kept. Lady her own housekeeper. Good wages to an efficient person, Address, stating full particulars, to W., Hollingbourne-house, Lower Norwood, Surrey.

COOK (thorough good) WANTED, in an hotel. Good character indispensable. Apply, between 10 and 4, at Ford's Hotel, Manchester-street, Manchester-square, W.

A Thoroughly good COOK WANTED, under a housekeeper, in a gentleman's family. Town and country. Between 30 and 35 years of age. Undeniable character required. Address A. H., Darman's Library, St. Leonard's-on-Sea.

GOOD COOK WANTED, in Surrey. Must understand ordering dinner. Dairy, baking. Large family. Wages £30. Address J733, Address and Inquiry office, The Times Office, E.C.

GOOD PLAIN COOK WANTED, in the country. Small family. Countrywoman preferred, over 30, clean, good manager. Wages £22, all found. Address Vicar, Epping.

GOOD PLAIN COOK WANTED. Churchwoman. Age 25 to 35. Some assistance given. Five children in family. Good personal character required. Wages £23, all found.—Mrs. Tidman, The Common, Chislehurst. At home after 4.

GOOD PLAIN COOK WANTED. Personal character. Not under 30. Small dairy. Kitchenmaid. 13 miles from London. Wages £25, and all found. State particulars. Address Mrs. Browell, Feltham, Middlesex.

PARLOURMAID for a gentleman's family in the country (Lincolnshire) REQUIRED at once. A little housework, with attendance on a lady. An excellent waitress. Good character and nice appearance indispensable. Height 5ft. 5. Age from 25. Wages £20, all found. Address E. M., Becklands, near Grimsby.

A Highly respectable YOUNG WOMAN WANTED, as PARLOURMAID. Age 25, tall, and a good character required.—Mrs. M., 134, Tulse-hill. S.W.

A HOUSE and PARLOUR MAID WANTED, about 27, in a gentleman's family of four. Wages £22, all found but beer. Apply 51, Chepstow-place, Pembridge-square, Bayswater.

GOOD HOUSE and PARLOUR MAID WANTED, in ladies' school, another housemaid kept. Age about 25. Wages £18 to £20, all found. Apply or write.—Miss Williams, York-house College, Kilburn Priory, London, N.W.

HOUSE and PARLOUR MAID REQUIRED, immediately, in a gentleman's small family. No man-servant. Wages £16, all found. Those with personal characters to apply at No. 14, Upper Brook-street, Grosvenor-square.

A First-rate UPPER HOUSEMAID WANTED, age 34 to 40; wages £20, beer £3, and all found. Also an Under Housemaid, age 22 to 25; wages £14, beer £3, and all found. Address Mrs. Barton Scobell, Kingwell-hall, near Bath.

'Situations Vacant' advertisements in The Times, *31 August 1880*

publishers of *The Times* encouraged servants to use its advertisement columns 'by arguing that it was to their advantage' to take a situation with employers who purchased an expensive newspaper.

The gentry did not often use newspapers to find new staff, but as Pamela Sambrook points out in *Keeping Their Place*, 'they would ask agencies to place discreetly worded adverts on their behalf.' Smaller households might place advertisements themselves, anonymously, and have the replies directed through the newspaper's office. This was the method used by Anne Boulton when she became mistress of her own house for the first time in December 1818. In *The Hardware Man's Daughter*, Shena Mason comments that when Anne needed new servants for her home at Thornhill, she advertised in *Aris's Gazette*. As a 50-year-old spinster, her household was far smaller than the one at Soho House where she had lived with her father Matthew, and later her brother, Matthew Robinson Boulton.

In 1820, Mary Galton wrote to her brother-in-law John Howard Galton about finding a housekeeper through a newspaper advertisement:

20 January 1820

We have succeeded in getting an excellent housekeeper for ourselves – she comes on Monday next; after waiting for some time I was advised by Mrs Norman and many others of my acquaintance to enquire after the good Advertisements, as the best Servants always advertise now; by these means I have procured Mrs Roberts. (MS 3101/C/D/10/7/4, Birmingham Archives and Heritage Service)

Servants' Registry Offices

The first servants' registry offices date back to the late eighteenth century, but it was in the Victorian period that they came into their own. They operated in the same way as employment agencies today. Such registries could be large or small organisations and were often run by men or women who had retired from domestic service themselves. Many registries were run in conjunction with another enterprise, for example a newsagent or stationer. The reputations of some servants' registry offices were suspect, with complaints being made about bogus job vacancies, while others, such as Mrs Hunt's Agency in London, catered for a higher standard of clientele and would only accept the best servants.

Some registries were run by charities such as the Girls' Friendly Society or the Metropolitan Association for Befriending Young Servants. The Domestic Servants' Benevolent Institution also ran a servants' registry. Its secretary wrote to the *Morning Chronicle* (1 October 1898) in response to 'The Domestic Servant Difficulty'. He pointed out the advantages of employers using the registry 'as it enables them to select servants of a class who, at any rate, have shown some prudence and benevolence towards their fellow servants in becoming members of the Institution. Moreover, no fees

'In a Servants' Registry Office: Servant London', Living London, 1902

whatever are charged to employers, whether they engage a servant or not.' The fact that fees were not charged to employers by this charity would have been a real incentive as they usually had to pay for the privilege of using a servants' registry.

Ladies wanting servants would contact a servants' registry office with their requirements, such as the type of servant and salary provided. These potential mistresses would do all they could to make their household stand out from the others – something that was especially evident in the late nineteenth and early twentieth centuries. Details in surviving registers often record information about holidays, the number of people in the household, and whether any servants were kept. 'No washing' or 'little washing' was almost universal by the 1890s since few servants were prepared to undertake the arduous task of the 'big wash'.

One piece of information which ladies often put in their advertisements at the registries (and in newspapers) was the length of time their previous servant had been with them. If it was more than a couple of years, this was a good indication to the prospective employee that the mistress was considerate and treated her staff well.

In *Keeping Their Place*, Pamela Sambrook comments that the Harpur Crewe family of Calke Abbey in Derbyshire relied heavily on domestic service agencies, but this was 'perhaps unusual'. They used a recruitment agency run by Mrs Moseley in Derby and the surviving correspondence between them spans twenty years.

'Outside a Registry Office: Servant London', Living London, *1902*

Servants applied to the registries for posts they were interested in. Fees varied, but usually both parties had to pay. In the 1870s, Hannah Cullwick found work through a servants' registry office at the Soho Bazaar. In *The Diaries of Hannah Cullwick: Victorian Maidservant,* edited by Elizabeth Stanley, she recalled she

> sat in the office with several more servants, young & old, waiting my turn for my name to be put down . . . I paid ½ a crown, the price for the lower servants – it's 5/- for cooks or upper ones. I was shown the way upstairs & where to wait . . . Then the ladies began to come in, & I felt very nervous til one lady spoke to me & she ask'd me to follow her, & that was to another room where the ladies sat & hir'd you or ask'd you questions after they'd walk'd round & pick'd you out.

The Importance of a Good 'Character'

To be able to move on to a place with higher pay or better prospects, servants needed a good 'character'. This was the reference which employers provided when a servant left a place, and it was always highlighted in newspaper advertisements placed by servants.

The importance of having a good 'character' or reference for moving on cannot be underestimated. However, as Trevor May points out in *The Victorian Domestic Servant*, employers were not obliged to provide a reference at all, 'but a false or defamatory one was only actionable at law if the servant could prove express malice, which it was virtually impossible to do.'

In a large country house, it was the senior servants who followed up references, not the master or mistress. Prospective new servants were interviewed and if successful, they were appointed subject to having a good character or testimonial. The new employer approached the previous employer in writing, asking for a reference. Unsuccessful interviewees were paid their expenses.

Margaret Powell was a cook in London in the 1920s. In her memoir *Below Stairs*, she commented: 'When you gave in your notice, you always tried to give the impression that you were loath to leave, you just had to make it seem that you were sorry to go. It was because of the reference; you couldn't get another job without a good reference.'

In her *Book of Household Management*, Mrs Beeton had these words of advice for mistresses giving a reference to former servants:

> In giving a character, it is scarcely necessary to say that the mistress should be guided by a sense of strict justice. It is not fair for one lady to recommend to another, a servant she would not keep herself. It is hardly necessary to remark, on the other hand, that no angry feelings on the part of a mistress towards her late servant, should ever be allowed, in the slightest degree, to influence her, so far as to induce her to disparage her maid's character.

She stressed that when engaging a servant,

> Every portion of work which the maid will have to do should be plainly stated by the mistress, and understood by the servant . . . If this plan is not carefully adhered to, domestic contention is almost certain to ensue, and this may not be easily settled; so that a change of servants, which is so much to be deprecated, is continually occurring.

In fact, a high proportion of servants regularly switched between employers searching for that elusive 'good place'. Miss Collet's *Report on the Money Wages of Indoor Domestic Servants* (1899) found that in London

36 per cent of servants had been in their current place for less than a year; the figure was 35 per cent in England and Wales (excluding London) and in Scotland, while it was 37 per cent in Ireland. For the same areas, the number in place for between three and four years was 10 per cent in London, England, Wales and Ireland; and 7 per cent in Scotland.

There were numerous reasons for seeking a new place with a different employer. In most cases, it was to secure a promotion or to receive better pay. Promotions within the same household were rare, hence the need to move between employers every couple of years. This was particularly the case for male servants, for whom there were less openings to begin with.

There was a natural progression between some roles. For example, a kitchen-maid, having gained sufficient experience in a large kitchen under a sympathetic cook who shared her skills, might move on to a first post as cook in a much smaller household. Equally, a footman might progress to a position as an under-butler, if he had ambitions to become a butler towards the end of his career.

A male servant, identified only with the initials 'E G', worked at Westbrook in Horsham, Sussex before moving on Bromley Palace in Kent. In January 1909, he sent a postcard of the house to his 'old chum' at Westbrook, C Taylor. In the message, he boasted that they 'all got a nice present' for Christmas: his was a solid silver match box. He also commented that Bromley Palace was much bigger than Westbrook as it had fifteen servants, and that a motor car was kept there, not horses. It is not clear what role E G was fulfilling, but he was probably a footman and was keen to say that, 'I get out every afternoon so it isn't so bad.'

For servants who wanted to experience a bit of life, London and other major cities and resorts were a strong magnet. Others moved to find better working conditions, more time off or perhaps to a situation where married couples were accepted.

The servant class was made up of those who made a career out of being in service and those who were marking time before marriage. According to Pamela Sambrook in *Keeping Their Place*, domestic service could be a 'good marriage market for girls – where else could they meet a variety of eligible young men, more exciting or exotic perhaps than those available from their own village?'

On leaving domestic service to get married, a female servant sacrificed both her independence and her income. She often ended up returning to the grinding poverty she had escaped from when she left her parents' home if she married within her own social class. This was especially the case if a large number of children then came along quickly.

In *Below Stairs*, Margaret Powell recalled how her mother encouraged her to go into domestic service in the 1920s:

> She forgot the tales she used to tell us – how she went into it when she was fourteen years old in 1895, and how she had to work like a galley slave; an object of derision to the other servants. [She] looked at her years in domestic service through a vista of married life, with a husband always out of work in the winter, with seven children and never enough money for food, never mind about clothes. Her years in domestic service seemed a time when at least she did have a certain amount of money that she could call her own.

Part 2

SERVANT LIFE

Chapter 5

WORKING CONDITIONS

The amount and type of work your servant ancestor was expected to do depended almost entirely on how many other staff were kept in the household. In a large country house, the hierarchy between servants was strictly maintained. They had very specific roles and worked in separate 'departments' of the house, and many of the tasks were divided between a number of different staff working in the same role. For instance, a head housemaid might have a second, third or even fourth housemaid working under her direction or a cook could be assisted by a kitchen-maid and scullery maid. The same was true of male servants with a butler in charge of an under-butler, first footman and second footman.

However, in the more common, smaller middle-class household, the distinction between roles was blurred and servants might have to undertake tasks they would not dream of doing in a larger place. A single-handed male servant in a small household might have the nominal title of butler, but he would have been carrying out the tasks associated with a butler, footman and valet combined, as well as plenty of arduous work usually assigned to a boot- or knife boy.

While the contemporary household manuals of the day such as Samuel and Sarah Adams's *The Complete Servant* and Isabella Beeton's *Book of Household Management* suggested the ideal routines and tasks for each servant, they were not meant to be taken literally. They were aspirational and every master or mistress took from them the most appropriate ideas and suggestions for their household, and adapted them to suit their individual circumstances.

For instance, Matthew Robinson Boulton, son of the industrialist Matthew Boulton, inherited Soho House in Birmingham when his father died in 1809. In 1813, he wrote a list of questions to be asked of applicants for the post of butler which included: 'Does the Butler understand the Duties of a Gentleman's own Man in such as laying out his Clothes & brushing them, & taking care generally of his Wardrobe & Shoes?' These duties were essentially those of a valet, indicating that Boulton was expecting his butler to perform both roles. These valet-related tasks did not appear on an earlier list of the butler's duties, which included 'Conveys messages & dispatches to the Manufactory'. Matthew Robinson Boulton was adamant that 'The old Cloathes [are] not to be counted as perquisites.' This would normally be a valuable extra for a valet. (MS 3782/13/149/72 Questions to be asked of Butler & Under Footman 1813, Birmingham Archives and Heritage Service)

Stringent rules were in place to control the lives of servants, especially in the large country houses. In *Keeping Their Place*, Pamela Sambrook quotes from the Regulations for Domestic Servants at Wimpole Hall, Cambridgeshire, circa 1790:

> No servant is to absent him or herself from the House for more than two hours at any time (& that only once a day) without asking leave thro their Butler or Housekeeper or Lady H. or myself; and no servant on any pretence whatsoever is to absent him or herself from meals, or from the house after 10 pm without special permission from either Lady H or myself. N.B. No perquisites are to be allowed to Servants.

Working Hours and Time Off

On the face of it, the relationship between masters and servants was an odd one. At the top of the scale, the wealthy gentry invited complete strangers to live in their homes, exposing them to all their secrets and tempting them with displays of wealth and extravagance. Indeed, nineteenth-century newspapers are full of reports about dishonest servants stealing from their employers. One would think that in this situation employers would have taken every opportunity to retain honest staff, instead of having to continually recruit new ones.

By making the accommodation as comfortable as possible and providing time off in which to rest or meet friends and relatives, an employer could make domestic service in his or her household attractive, even if a high salary could not be afforded. However, during the nineteenth century, this appears to have been the exception rather than the rule.

The main complaint voiced by servants was about the long working hours, coupled with lack of time off for leisure activities and rest. Unsurprisingly, it was also the main reason alternatives to domestic service were chosen by girls who would formerly have considered no other occupation.

Advertisement for Brooke's Soap, The Illustrated London News, *26 April 1890*

From the Georgian period onwards, the use of non-electric wire-operated bells meant that the servant's work was constantly interrupted, often for petty reasons. In *What the Butler Winked At*, Eric Horne commented:

The shop girl or factory girl may have to work hard, but she does not have to begin work at five-thirty and keep on more or less continually till ten-thirty at night, as I know of some housemaids who do it in the winter. The outdoor girl can look forward to the time she will finish for the day, probably at five or six in the evening. The employer does not trouble himself what they do or where they go; as soon as they are outside the place, they are free.

A servant named only as 'Fellow Sufferer' wrote to the *Star of Gwent* (21 November 1890) to complain of the long hours she and her fellow servants had to work: 'Many girls are on from six thirty in the morning until eleven or twelve o'clock at night . . . I say life is not worth living if things are going on at this rate. Slaves we are called, a more suitable name could not be found.'

Servants working for the gentry found their hours increased considerably during the London season because there was so much evening work in addition to the usual day chores. Eric Horne recalled being in service as a footman to a baron. He and another footman had to accompany the carriage whenever their master went out to dinner or other function.

They would keep us out regularly till one, two or three o'clock, but we had to start work at the same time as the other servants. Often during the London season we were kept so short of our hours of sleep that I used to go to sleep on the carriage; the coachman would notice it and draw the handle of his knotty whip under my nose. I would wake up with a start, and wonder where I was. One footman, who lived near us in the country, went to sleep on the box of a high barouche, and actually fell backwards, and landed among the ladies.

In the eighteenth and early nineteenth centuries, very few servants had any formally recognised time off, except for going to church. This applied particularly to female servants and junior men-servants. The situation started to improve by the end of the nineteenth century and the beginning of the twentieth, when it was more common for servants to have at least a day off once a month.

Margaret Thomas remembered her first position as housemaid in the 1900s in *The Day Before Yesterday*, edited by Noel Streatfeild: 'I never had any settled hours off, except on Sundays to go to church, morning one week and evening the next; once a month we all had a day off. We left on Sunday and came back the next night, or we could wait two or three months and have longer.'

By this time, formalised days off and time for holidays were used to attract servants to positions. It was easier to grant holidays in large country houses where numerous servants were kept. Staff might be allowed a week's or a fortnight's holiday, which could be taken when the family was away, taking turns with the other servants.

Miss Collet's *Report on the Money Wages of Indoor Domestic Servants* (1899) discovered that '. . . mistresses employing only one or two servants make mention much more frequently than others of the special privileges and holidays granted by them. The difficulty of obtaining servants is much greater in such households, and holidays and privileges are therefore offered as an inducement instead of high wages, which the mistresses cannot afford to pay.' When granting holidays to their servants, these mistresses suffered a 'much greater personal inconvenience' because the work had to be 'performed by the mistress or her family or by a charwoman requiring extra pay.'

The maximum holiday given in any one case was 'A fortnight in summer, one day monthly, half day every Sunday, evening out weekly'. The *Report* concluded that: 'The evening a week is given in most cases as well as the Sunday evening; and the one day a month is also common.'

Miss Collet was pleased to find that 'In a few instances it is stated that the servant may receive her friends one evening a week, and in one household, each of the three servants is allowed one evening a week separately for receiving her own friends.'

When servants did have time off, they would visit friends and family if they lived close enough, or go into the nearest town or village. If they were in service at a country house, walks and other outdoor pursuits were popular. Although footmen were no longer required to run alongside carriages, they still needed to be physically fit. According to Pamela Sambrook in *Keeping Their Place*, many country houses staged regular foot races for their servants, while other male servants might enjoy outdoor sports such as badger baiting, cock fighting or 'sparring'.

In large households where a good number of staff were kept, employers threw an annual ball for the servants to thank them for their hard work. More benevolent employers allowed their staff to hold regular, informal monthly dances.

The bicycle was an important possession for Edwardian servants, especially if they lived in a remote country household, since it represented freedom and allowed them to remain in contact with friends and family. In *Yes, Ma'am! Glimpses of Domestic Service 1901–1951*, M C Scott-Moncrieff quotes from the memories of Isabella (Bella) Anderson who first went into service in about 1910. She was the eldest of seven children and her father was a foreman on a farm in the north of Fife. When she was 16, she was offered a place by an unmarried lady from Newport (the nearest town) on the condition that she had a 'trunk, three wrappers and an afternoon black dress; caps, shoes and aprons, all new'.

Bella recalled:

> The lady was very kind. I was well fed and was paid £14 a year. I only got home once a month for the day and a weekend every three months. I was terribly homesick until I'd saved enough to buy a second-hand bicycle. Then home every Sunday after the dinner dishes were done but had to be in by nine o'clock.

Her home was seventeen miles from Newport. In addition, she was allowed to go to church two Sundays out of three. 'I also got out on Saturday after tea and having been at school in that district, I had two school friends and an old aunt of my father's to go to.'

Attitudes of Employers Towards Servants

When employers showed kindness and consideration towards their servants, it was always appreciated and often resulted in loyal service over many years. On many of the large country estates, there were countless examples of servants working for one master for twenty years or more. On 13 December 1856, the *Wrexham and Denbighshire Weekly Advertiser* reported on the funeral of 'Thomas Fitzhugh Esquire of Plas Power'. It highlighted the large number of long-serving servants on his staff, including Robert Hughes who had served fifty-nine years. The newspaper commented: 'A kind master must be a good and kind man, and when we find a servant serving one master for 59 years, it is equally creditable to both.'

Other long-serving members of staff were Mr Barnes (butler), thirty-three years; Mr J Cotton (groom), thirty years; Mr Ellison (gardener), twenty-seven years; Mrs Lightfoot (cook), twenty-seven years; Mrs Davies (housekeeper), twenty-six years; and Mrs Cornill (lady's maid), twenty-six years. Unsurprisingly, five years later when the 1861 census was taken, none of these servants were still at Plas Power. The death of an employer usually brought about a 'changing of the guard' because whoever inherited the estate had their own staff, who they brought with them.

Amongst benevolent employers, there was a strong desire to help improve their servants' education or skills. In *The Victorian House*, Judith

'Laying and Lighting a Fire: Housewifery Lessons under the London School Board', The Illustrated London News, *4 March 1893*

Flanders quotes the example of Geraldine Jewsbury, a Manchester novelist who heard about a position as lady's maid that might suit her housemaid. She 'went and interviewed the lady herself to promote her maid's case, gave the maid a week off to go and learn the one skill she was missing, and arranged for her own milliner to teach her quilling and cap-making.'

Before her marriage, Mrs Wrigley, 'A Plate Layer's Wife', worked in domestic service. Her third situation in 1872 was in Oldham at a Temperance Hotel. She was then 14 years old and she recorded the kindness of her new employers in her memoir in *Life As We Have Known It*: 'Seeing as I could not read or write, my master and mistress took an interest in me and paid for my education at the night school for two years. He also helped me at night with my lessons. They proved a father and mother to me.'

In her final place before she married, Mrs Wrigley found herself as cook in 'the very best place I had in all my life'. She recalled:

We had plenty of freedom, going out in our turn. We were not treated as servants but as all one family, and with respect. The servants was thought so much of, and when we had a ball the kitchen staff was allowed to have one dance with the guests. My master and mistress [were] real Christian and she was the kindest lady in the village. Everybody was alike to her, but she had her house rule kept in order. Not one of us was allowed out one minute after nine o'clock. The bell rang out 'all in', but the girls loved her too much to disobey her. I was there five years, and married from there. I was sorry to give up such a good home . . .

Mrs Layton, another servant whose story is told in *Life As We Have Known It*, was discouraged by one employer from reading books, but at her next place, the attitude of her mistress was very different:

In this household, reading was not considered a waste of time, and books were supplied to me to read which were suitable to a young impressionable girl, far different to the trash I had read in secret before. I was encouraged to improve my education. I used to write and my mistress would correct the mistakes in spelling and grammar.

This employer also allowed her to go out every evening after the six o'clock dinner was served, as long as she was back by nine o'clock.

In *Below Stairs*, Margaret Powell worked as a temporary cook in the 1920s for a very kind employer:

They were the most thoughtful and kind people I'd ever met, ever since I'd started in domestic service. They spoke to us in exactly the same way that they would speak to people of their own society . . . And it was the first place *I'd* been in where the people above – 'Them' – called you by your Christian name . . . And when it was the servants' birthdays they all had lovely presents, not print dresses, black stockings, and caps . . . but real presents.

For her birthday, Margaret was given 'beautiful silk underwear, the sort of thing I'd never been able to buy. Yet I'd only been there six weeks and she knew I was only going to stay three months . . .'

Present buying like this was extremely rare, except from the most considerate employers. In most large households, Christmas presents for the servants were usually graded according to their status, but were not personalised; they were work-related gifts such as a new uniform.

In her *Book of Household Management*, Mrs Beeton recommended that 'using a proper amount of care in choosing servants, and treating them like reasonable beings, and making slight excuses for the shortcomings of human nature' would mean that employers would 'save in some exceptional case, be tolerably well served, and, in most instances, surround themselves with attached domestics.'

Sadly, not all employers followed Mrs Beeton's advice to treat their servants 'like reasonable beings'. Youngsters going into service for the first time were particularly vulnerable to exploitation, cruelty and neglect. There were many high-profile cases of extreme neglect or mistreatment leading to the deaths of servants, such as Mary Parsons in 1849 and Emily Jane Popejoy in 1897, and also cases in which the servant's life was saved just in time, such as Jane Wilbred in 1850. However, there were doubtless many other instances of beatings, bullying and general cruelty to servants which went unreported.

Personal Relationships of Servants

Although most employers allowed servants to entertain members of their family for a meal in the household, the same invitations did not extend to friends or servants from other houses. Employers wanted to prevent the spread of gossip about the household at all costs. However, as Trevor May points out in *The Victorian Domestic Servant*, it was difficult to do this 'when downstairs had its own access to the street via a door into the sub-pavement area.'

'Followers' were actively discouraged, not just on moral grounds. In *Keeping Their Place,* Pamela Sambrook comments that 'Food and drink could be lavished on them and some servants certainly made free with their employer's hospitality.'

As Margaret Powell points out in *Below Stairs*:

If you left to get married . . . it was acceptable and it was respectable. And yet the business of getting a young man was not respectable, and one's employers tended to degrade any relationship. It seemed to me one was expected to find husbands under a gooseberry bush. Their daughters were debs, and they could meet young men at balls, dances and private parties, but if any of the servants had boyfriends they were known as 'followers' . . . it brings to your mind people slinking through back streets, not seeing the light of day, with any young man that cares for you . . . They made you feel that there was something intrinsically bad in having a member of the opposite sex interested in you at all.

Postcard of an unidentified under-nurse with the children she was looking after on the Isle of Wight, circa 1905. Author's collection

Margaret Thomas worked in service in the early 1900s. In *The Day Before Yesterday* she recalled she was 'allowed to be friends with the outdoor staff, but if indoor servants were found to be keeping company the girl was instantly dismissed. I thought this was most unfair on us girls, no wonder footmen were always so conceited.'

These were the usual double standards in Victorian society and they also applied if a servant girl found herself pregnant. She was told to leave immediately but a similar punishment was rarely meted out to the father, who may have been another servant or even a member of the family she served. If the girl had no family to turn to, her future was bleak. She could live on her meagre savings for a while, but once they ran out, there was no choice but to apply to the workhouse for poor relief. Many desperate servants tried to end their pregnancies, and if this failed, some took the difficult decision to place their children in the care of a charity, such as the Foundling Hospital.

Although relationships between members of domestic staff were actively discouraged by employers, they were inevitable in country houses in remote areas where servants worked closely together and had little opportunity to meet other people.

Born in 1820 in Warwick, by the age of 47, John Pitchford had been employed as butler at Eden Hall, Cumberland for at least sixteen years. It is not known when he was appointed, but he was listed there on both the 1851 and 1861 censuses.

Also on the staff for the same period of time was Elizabeth Nott, who worked as lady's maid. She was four years older than John and came from Colwall in Herefordshire. As both were members of the senior staff, they would have had plenty of time to get to know each other in the so-called 'Pug's Parlour' where the upper servants ate supper together separately from the other members of staff.

John and Elizabeth eventually married but it is not clear at what point they began their relationship. Perhaps John was worried about damaging his career prospects, or Elizabeth was reluctant to lose her independence. At 51, she was past her childbearing years so having a family was not the motive behind their marriage. In his late forties, John had not yet reached retirement age, but he had possibly come to the stage where he no longer wanted to be tied to domestic service. Perhaps they had found a kindred spirit in one another and wanted companionship in later life.

Their wedding did not take place until November 1867 when they married by licence at the parish church in Penrith. Elizabeth's residence was listed as Eden Hall and John was living in Arthur Street, Penrith. His father was named as Richard Pitchford, a gentleman's servant, while Elizabeth was the daughter of William Nott, a farmer.

Whatever the reasons for their marriage, they were together for twenty-seven years before Elizabeth died in 1884. John died six years later, leaving a personal estate of £3,161 19s 6d, and described in his will as a 'gentleman'.

Chapter 6

WAGES

The rate of pay a servant received depended to a large extent on his or her experience, and the social position of the employer. Those with a greater number of years' service could ask for higher wages than less-experienced servants. More generous wages were also paid in town than in the countryside, except if working for the nobility on a landed estate. As a general rule, the larger the establishment, the higher the wages a servant could expect.

In addition to a salary, servants' contracts might include allowances for beer, tea and sugar. Some servants could also supplement their salary with valuable perquisites, and tips or 'vails'.

Rates of Pay

The terms on which wages were paid to servants related directly to the 1662 Settlement and Removal Act. This legislation stipulated that workers from outside a parish could only gain settlement, and therefore have the right to poor relief, if they were employed for over a year.

Employers were usually ratepayers who funded poor relief so it was in their interests to avoid claims for settlement. To do this, they signed their servants on for fifty-one weeks, with the final week of the year as an unofficial holiday. Servants were paid in arrears after they had worked for the period in their contract, i.e. after they had worked for a year.

By the mid- to late nineteenth century, it was more common for servants to be paid half-yearly or quarterly. Whatever terms a servant was employed on, he or she could always apply for an advance from their employer. If servants were satisfactory at the end of the agreement, they were signed on for another year; if not, they were given notice to leave.

In a country house when the family was away from home, perhaps spending the season in London, the servants who did not go with them were paid board wages. This was an allowance of money in lieu of meals, meaning that servants had to buy their own food. For male servants particularly, it could be difficult to get hot meals when board wages were paid. Kitchen staff would probably have saved money by clubbing together to make their meals.

The following tables give an indication of recommended annual salaries for servants across the nineteenth century, although only Miss Collet's *Report* includes actual wages paid. In larger households, there were often 'upper' and 'under' servants, and when roles were combined, the job titles changed as reflected in the tables.

ANNUAL WAGES OF MALE DOMESTIC SERVANTS

	Samuel and Sarah Adams's *The Complete Servant* (1825) – recommended annual wages	Mrs Beeton's *Book of Household Management* (1861) – recommended annual wages		The Servants' Practical Guide (1880) – recommended annual wages	Board of Trade surveys from Miss Collet's *Report* (1894–8) – actual average annual wages	
		When not found in livery	When found in livery		Average Wages	Number in Return
House steward	£100–£250	£40–£80	—		—	—
Butler	£50–£80 in large families, £30–£50 in smaller families	£25–£50	—	£50–£80	£58.6	85
Under-butler	16g–25g	£15–£30	£15–£25		—	—
Valet	£30–£60	£25–£50	£20–£30		—	—
Man-cook	—	£20–£40	—		£128.0	2
Footman	20g–30g	£20–£40	£15–£25	£14–£28	£26.7	84
Under-footman	16g–20g	—	£12–£20		—	—
Coachman	25g–36g	—	£20–£35	16s–25s pw	—	—
Groom	£22–£25	£15–£30	£12–£20	10s–18s pw	—	—
Steward's room boy	£8–£12	—	—		—	—
Page/foot-boy or hall-boy	—	£8–£18	£6–£14		—	—
Stable-boy	£8–£21	£6–£12	—		—	—
Gardener	£50–£100	£20–£40	—		—	—
Men-servants (duties undefined)	—	—	—		£38.6	31
Boy	—	—	—		£10.9	28

1 guinea (g) = £1 1s 0d
£1 = 20 shillings
1 shilling (s) = 12 pence

ANNUAL WAGES OF FEMALE DOMESTIC SERVANTS

	Samuel and Sarah Adams's *The Complete Servant* (1825) – recommended annual wages	Mrs Beeton's *Book of Household Management* (1861) – recommended annual wages		*The Servants' Practical Guide* (1880) – recomm. annual wages	Board of Trade surveys from Miss Collet's *Report* (1894–8) – actual average annual wages from 2,000+ households			
		No allow. for tea, sugar and beer	Allow. for tea, sugar and beer		London	England & Wales inc London	Scotland	Ireland
Housekeeper	25g–50g	£20–£45	£18–£20	—	£34.3	£52.2	£45.0	—
Lady's maid	18g–25g	£12–£25	£10–£20	£20–£35	£28.1	£24.7	£24.4	£24.0
Cook	—	£14–£30	£12–£26		£21.8	£20.2	£20.6	£17.2
Cook (professed)				£50–£70				
Cook (plain)				£16–£30				
Cook-housekeeper	—	—	—		£41.6	£35.6	£22.0	—
Upper housemaid	12g–16g	£12–£20	£10–£17		—	—	—	—
Under housemaid	£10–£12	£8–£12	£6½–£10		—	—	—	—
Housemaid	—	—	—	£12–£30	£17.5	£16.2	£17.1	£13.5
Parlourmaid	—	—	—		£22.2	£20.6	£20.1	£16.0
Upper laundry-maid	—	£12–£18	£10–£15		—	—	—	—
Under laundry-maid	—	£9–£14	£8–£12		—	—	—	—
Laundry-maid	£8–£15	—	—		£27.3	£23.6	£20.0	—
Dairymaid	£8–£12	—	—		—	—	—	—
Maid of all work/ general servant	8g–12g	£9–£14	£7½–£11		£14.9	£14.6	£15.3	£10.3
Stillroom-maid	8g–12g	£9–£14	£8–£12		—	—	—	—
Head nurse	18g–25g	£15–£30	£13–£26	£20–£25	—	—	—	—
Nurse	—	—	—		£21.0	£20.1	£19.5	£15.8
Under-nurse	10g–12g	—	—		—	—	—	—
Nurse-maid	6g–10g	£8–£12	£5–£10	£10–£14	—	—	—	—
Nurse-housemaid	—	—	—		£14.9	£16.0	£14.0	—
Kitchen-maid	12g–14g	£9–£14	£8–£12	£14–£28	£16.6	£15.0	£15.0	£11.3
Scullery maid	8g–12g	£5–£9	£4–£8	£12–£18	£13.7	£13.0	—	—
Between maid	—	—	—		£12.4	£10.7	—	—

1 guinea (g) = £1 1s 0d
£1 = 20 shillings
1 shilling (s) = 12 pence

There were regional differences in salaries, and even in different areas of London. In *The Victorian Domestic Servant*, Trevor May quotes Charles Booth's figures from *Life and Labour of the People of London* which stated the average wage of a housemaid in the West End of London was £17, while in the East End it was only £13.

In 1899, Miss Collet's *Report on the Money Wages of Indoor Domestic Servants* concluded that 'the rate of wages paid in large households by no means represent the average paid in all households large and small.' The report found that the average money wages of female indoor servants was £17 6s in London; £15 10s in the rest of England and Wales; and £17 6s in the three principal Scottish cities (Glasgow, Edinburgh and Dundee).

This contrasted with the average wages for a butler at £58 6s; a footman £26 7s; a general man-servant £38 6s; a boy £10 9s; and a man-cook £128.

A first position in service was poorly paid because of the relatively young age of applicants and the distinct lack of experience. In London, under the Metropolitan Association for Befriending Young Servants (MABYS) system, the average initial wage for girls under 15 was £5 9s.

On landed estates, wages were roughly similar from place to place. In the 1820s at Himley Hall in Staffordshire, the seat of Lord Dudley, the housekeeper (who doubled as the cook) was paid £47 5s a year. The footman and the groom received £24 3s, while the gardener was paid £52 10s. The upper housemaid received £12 12s; the under-housemaid £10 10s; the upper stillroom maid £10 10s; the under stillroom maid £8 8s; the upper dairymaid £11 11s and the under dairymaid £10 10s. (DE/IV/10/2 Ledgers 1817–1823, Dudley Archives and Local History Service)

In the 1830s at Eden Hall, Cumbria, wages receipts show that the footman was paid £21 a year, the stillroom maid £9, the butler £63 16s and one of the housemaids received £9 a year. At Eden Hall, the laundry-maid was paid substantially more than the housemaids at £17 a year, presumably because the work was so heavy. By 1869, the wages for the butler had not increased much at £65 a year, but the housemaids' wages had. The head housemaid was paid £20 a year; the second £16; the third £12; and the kitchen-maid received £18 a year. The cook was paid £50 while the coachman was on £27 6s a year.

By contrast, at Erddig, Denbighshire, the servants were paid well below the average wages for country house posts. According to Merlin Waterson in *The Servants' Hall: The Domestic History of a Country House*, in 1903, the butler was paid £55 a year while 'the junior maids at Erddig were receiving between

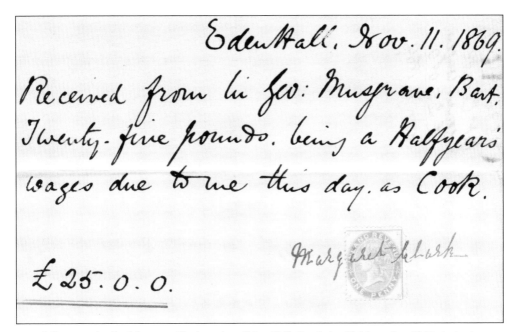

Wages receipt for Margaret Clark, cook at Eden Hall, Cumbria, 11 November 1869. Author's collection

£8 and £15.' However, he argues that comparisons with the salaries of other country houses 'ought to be seen in the context of the quality of food and accommodation offered.'

The industrialist Matthew Boulton lived at Soho House in Birmingham from 1766 until his death in 1809, after which the property was inherited by his son, Matthew Robinson Boulton. According to Shena Mason in the *Soho House Guide*, in 1801 Matthew Boulton kept four male servants as well as three female servants. Like other masters, he had difficulty finding and keeping good servants, partly because he was widowed and much of his time was taken up at his manufactory.

Records survive of the wages paid to Matthew Boulton's servants from 1788 onwards. One unusual agreement was made in January 1798 when Boulton appointed James Burford and it seems the terms were devised specifically to induce James to stay at Soho, with incremental salary increases each year.

Boulton agreed 'To allow him for the 1st year (1798) £8 8s, 2nd year (1799) £9 9s, 3rd year (1800) £10 10s, 4th year (1801) £11 11s, 5th year (1802) £12 12s.' There was also 'One Guinea a Year in addition for washing and his usual

Liveries including a Hat, also a Grt [Great] Coat & a Pair of Boots every Two Years but he must find himself Shoes, Shirts, Stockings &c.' The fact that liveries are mentioned tends to suggest James Burford was probably a footman.

It appears that he had little money at the time of his employment as 'At the commencement of this Agreement, Mr Boulton gave Jas. Burford a compleat Stock of Cloathes, of all description & 10 Guineas to begin the World with & as an encouragement to frugality has agreed to allow him 5 P C int. [interest] on any money not drawn in regular course but left in Mr Boulton's hands.' It is not known if this inducement encouraged Burford to stay at Soho or whether he was more frugal as a result. (MS 3782/6/101, Servants' Wages 1788–1805, Birmingham Archives and Heritage Service)

Offering a servant 5 per cent interest on any wages he did not spend was an unusual arrangement, although not unheard of. In *Keeping Their Place*, Pamela Sambrook cites James Tomlin, an under-butler promoted to butler in 1818, who served the Leicester-Warren family of Tabley Hall, Cheshire. As butler, he earned £52 10s per year. The wages book shows that 'not only was he receiving interest on a loan of £230 he had previously made to his employer, but for the three years as butler he asked the family to save his wages and allowances for him, thereby earning extra interest at 5 per cent.'

Matthew Robinson Boulton took a leaf out of his father's book when trying to encourage his servants to stay with him at Soho House. On 14 August 1830, he appointed George Horwood as groom, but the terms under which he was employed may mean he was serving out some kind of apprenticeship.

In the first year, he was to receive 'Cloathes, Washing & Maintenance Only'; in the second year 'Washing & Linen with £5 5 0 wages', followed in the third year with 'Washing & £8 8 0 wages'. In addition, he was allowed '1 Suit of Livery, 1 Stable Dress complete, 1 pair of Boots and 1 Hat [all] per annum, [and] 1 Great Coat once in 2 Years'. When ordered, his new clothes were 'found to be much needed'. It is not known how long this arrangement lasted. (MS 3782/13/149/94, Birmingham Archives & Heritage Service)

In 1835, the liveried servants at Soho House were paid slightly less than country house staff but the property was a much smaller establishment. The coachman was paid £24 3s per annum while the footman received £21 the first year and £23 in the second year. Both received liveries. (MS 3782/6/104 Servants Liveries 1834–5, Birmingham Archives and Heritage Service)

It was customary for the landed gentry to grant their servants a sum of money when they left service to get married – provided they did not leave

'Between the Dances: Dancing London', Living London, *1902*

under a cloud! In the salaries ledger for Himley Hall, Staffordshire, on 6 February 1819 there was an entry for 'Lucy Cutler (late Fellows)', meaning that her maiden name had been Fellows and that she had recently married. She was an under-housemaid and received her year's wages in arrears on 1 May. On 14 August, it was recorded that Lucy Cutler was granted 'an additl. half Yrs. Wages as a Gratuity by his Lordships order'. (DE/IV/10/2 Ledgers 1817–1823, Dudley Archives and Local History Service)

Gratuities were also paid to reward good service. On 24 July 1813 Elizabeth Walker, Sarah Southall and Eliza Hitchcock all had gratuities added to their year's wages. Elizabeth was the housekeeper on a salary of £42, and she had an extra £5 5s. Sarah was the stillroom maid and Eliza was the housemaid and they were both paid £8 8s a year. Their gratuity was £2 2s each. (DE/IV/10/1 Ledgers 1796–1817, Dudley Archives and Local History Service)

In July 1805, Rebecca Richards was appointed as a maid at Soho House in Birmingham for the Boulton family. The exact nature of her work was probably as lady's maid to Anne Boulton for it was agreed to pay her '£8 8s 0 a year & to be paid for learning to dress hair'. The ability to dress hair in all manner of different ways was an essential attribute for a lady's maid. It appears that Rebecca was appointed at a slightly lower wage than if she had already possessed hairdressing skills, but that Anne was prepared to invest in training her. By 1807, a new lady's maid, Ann Loxley, was appointed at £10 10s a year. (MS 3782/6/102, Servants' Wages 1801–1810, Birmingham Archives and Heritage Service)

Although the rate of wages was important when choosing a position, this was not the only consideration. Miss Collet's *Report* concluded that 'The quality of the food and lodging provided, the amount of work to be done, the household organisation, and the efficiency and personal characteristics of both mistress and servant are the most important factors in determining the advantages and disadvantages of a situation.'

For some older servants, especially females for whom marriage was no longer an option, a good place was more important than a high salary as shown in this advertisement from *The Bristol Mercury and Daily Post* (10 September 1886):

> WANTED Situation as PLAIN COOK, age 31, in small family. Wages not so much an object as comfortable home. Good reference. Address – A. Hill, Quarry, Dursley, Gloucestershire.

As Geoffrey Best points out in *Mid-Victorian Britain 1851–1875*, the female servant 'would also have the chance, not generally available to unmarried working women outside the cotton counties, to amass those savings which might so powerfully attract offers of marriage.'

With board and lodging provided, there were real opportunities for domestic servants to save significant sums of money. Unfortunately, having such savings could easily attract offers from the wrong kind of man, as shown in a London court case in December 1881. Ellen Holley, 25 years old and 'a fresh, pretty girl', was employed as a housemaid at a fashionable residence in Park Lane, where she had worked for six years. She was swindled out of her life savings by Henry Cook, a dancing master using the alias of Pearson. Various newspapers reported on the case including *The Times* (11 January

'A Nice General Servant', The Illustrated Police News, *8 June 1872*

1882). Henry Cook was a 'well-dressed man, wearing a heavy moustache and with hair beginning to turn grey'. He met Ellen when she was leaving church one Sunday evening and struck up a conversation with her. After winning her trust, he asked her to go for a walk with him, at which point he told her he earned £4 10s per week, had shares in the Great Northern Railway, and that his employer was anxious he should get married.

The following Sunday, Ellen met Henry again. He told her he wanted to give her his photograph and asked if she had any jewellery he could put it in. Trustingly, she gave him her gold watch worth £6 10s to borrow, which he was to return to her the following week. A week later, he did not have the watch with him but he pledged to marry her. Shortly afterwards, he told her he had been security for a friend and the loan office was pressing him for payments. He asked Ellen how much money she had with her, and how much she had altogether. She replied she only had £5 on her person, and £47 in the Post Office Savings Bank. Ellen decided to give Henry the £5, and she subsequently met him a few days later at the house where she worked and gave him £40. Henry failed to keep their next appointment, and Ellen enquired about him at the place where he said he was employed. It was at this point she discovered that Henry had used an alias.

As the *Western Mail* reported, 'Instead . . . of sitting down and weeping and wringing her hands, fair Ellen . . . put the matter into the hands of the police, with the excellent result that Cook, alias Pearson, was shortly afterwards arrested.'

When Henry Cook first appeared before magistrates in December 1881, the *Western Mail* published an article headed 'Housemaids and their Dangers' which berated mistresses for not taking a 'direct interest in the affairs of their maids, who devoid of experience and friends to advise them, frequently become involved in intrigues of the true nature of which they are entirely ignorant; or fall an easy prey of thieves and scoundrels'. It continued: 'Many a piteous tale of sorrow and misery would remain untold if ladies took more interest in the affairs of their servants, allowed them to visit their friends more frequently; and acted towards them more like a friend and less like a biped of a superior species.'

The case was referred to the Central Criminal Court in January 1882 when it was discovered that Ellen Holley was just one of Henry Cook's many victims, and that he had a wife and six children. He was only indicted by three other servants from whom he had obtained money and jewellery – Cornelia Willis, Ellen Stone and Lena Kenzel – but the police knew of twenty similar cases. It was reported that: 'in one instance a respectable young woman had been so deceived by the representations of the prisoner that she left a good situation under the idea that he was going to marry her, and the result was that she was utterly ruined.'

Addressing the jury, the barrister for the defence 'declared that the foolish young women who had allowed the prisoner to stop and speak to them were entitled to very little sympathy. The fact was they parted with their jewellery because they wanted to get married.'

Nevertheless, Henry Cook was convicted of obtaining money and jewellery by false pretences and sentenced to five years' penal servitude. For Ellen Holley, justice was done but her life savings could not be recovered. She was still single at the time of the 1891 census, working as a cook for an American journalist, and it is not known if she ever married.

An engraving of a lady in her chamber with her lady's maid at Sizergh Hall, Westmorland, dated 1845. Author's collection

Allowances

Allowances for beer, tea and sugar were often part of a servant's contract with an employer, and might also include candles, soap and laundry. When allowances were not made for these expensive commodities, this could lead to resentment among servants and to them simply helping themselves. This happened to Elizabeth Shackleton, mistress at Alkincoats, who, according to Amanda Vickery in *The Gentlemen's Daughter: Women's Lives in Georgian England*, made no allowance for tea, coffee and sugar in her servants' contracts, and the 'expropriation of illegitimate perquisites threatened both [her] authority and her economical regime.' In 1779, after finding 'Betty Crooke Making Coffee & breaking white sugar to drink with it', Elizabeth commented: 'Servants come to a high hand indeed. What will become of poor House Keepers?'

In the eighteenth century, grey wigs were still fashionable and were a required part of the uniform of a senior servant. A tradition of powdering the hair of liveried footmen developed from this and continued into the twentieth century, although the process was very unpopular. Some employers provided powder for their footmen and butlers, while others gave an allowance of powder money.

Beer money, and the availability of alcohol, had a detrimental effect on the well-being of countless servants who developed drink problems. Writing in the *Cornhill Magazine* (July 1901), Mrs Earle advised that 'the beer money, instead of being paid weekly, should be added to the wages and paid quarterly.' She added: 'If masters and mistresses only realised the number of young servants who have been taught to drink by being tempted to take the spirits on the cold grey morning when they come to their work, masters and mistresses would be more careful to lock away the whisky and brandy before they go to bed.'

According to *The Servants' Practical Guide* of 1880, if tea and sugar was given as an allowance, the usual quantity allowed to each servant was '1 lb of tea per month, and 2 lbs of loaf sugar, or money to this equivalent'. Beer money varied from 1s 6d to 2s 6d per week and 'in some households the under female servants are allowed but 1s per week.'

In 1855, Agnes Blundell, the mistress of Crosby Hall in Liverpool, wrote in her diary the names of the servants she had hired that year, and the terms:

> May 25th Elizabeth Young entered my service at £8 per annum & I am to find her tea, sugar & washing
> Mrs Gaily at £20 per annum [probably the cook]
> Ann Barker at £9 per annum
> [John] Murphy at £18 per annum
> [Elizabeth] Allen at £16 finding her tea, sugar & washing from the 29th of October [possibly a lady's maid]
> Jannette at £6 finding her tea, sugar & washing from the 12th of September
>
> (DDBL 53/57 Diary for 1855, Lancashire Archives)

Elizabeth Young had travelled from Taunton to Crosby for which she was reimbursed £1 14s. By 1861, only Elizabeth Allen, the lady's maid, was still employed by the Blundells although the number of servants they kept had increased considerably. In addition to Elizabeth Allen, there was a butler, footman, cook and groom; another lady's maid and a housekeeper; a monthly nurse, two nurses, a nursery maid and a governess; two housemaids, a kitchen-maid, scullery maid, dairymaid and laundry-maid. The Blundells, who were a Catholic family, employed a man-cook as part of their staff.

Perquisites

Perquisites were used goods which could be sold for cash and made a valuable addition to a servant's salary. They ranged from grease for cooks, corks for butlers, clothing for valets and ladies' maids, and rabbit skins for scullery maids.

In *Every Other Sunday: The Autobiography of a Kitchen-maid*, Jean Rennie recalled: 'An old travelling packman came round every week, and for each rabbit skin he gave me fourpence and for each hare skin a shilling. But they had to be really nicely skinned and not broken.'

Tips

In large households, tips, also known as 'vails', were expected from house-guests as a servant's right. They were substantial amounts of money, prompting an unsuccessful campaign in the eighteenth century to abolish 'taking the vail'.

Cooks earned commission from tradesmen, but in most cases, tips and Christmas boxes were reserved for male servants such as footmen and valets. Miss Collet discovered in her 1899 *Report* that 'The majority of adult male indoor servants are in large households employing over six servants, and the vails received by them are a very much larger item in their earning than in the case of women in such households.'

Chapter 7

FOOD AND DRINK

Food

Food and drink were provided for servants as part of their contract with their employer. However, the quantity of food was dependent on the servants' allowances given by the mistress to the cook. In *The Victorian Domestic Servant*, Trevor May argues that 'there is widespread agreement that [servants] ate at least as well as most members of the working class and enjoyed more meat than others of a similar situation.'

In a large country house where food was in abundance, this must have been a great improvement for those who had come from impoverished homes. The food was simple, and according to Pamela Sambrook in *Keeping Their Place*, servants ate 'stews using poorer cuts of meat or offal, or roast meat served up cold again and again'. However, meals were supplemented with home-grown fruit and vegetables from the kitchen garden. In smaller households, food may have been less plentiful and even insufficient, particularly in places where just one servant was kept.

The quantities of meat given to servants provoked criticism from some quarters. It was believed they were being spoiled because, had they remained with their working-class brothers and sisters living independently, they would only be able to afford meat perhaps once or twice a week. A correspondent to the *Pall Mall Gazette* (24 May 1865) warned employers about over-indulging their servants:

> Boys and girls taken into service from the village school, whose parents rarely eat meat more than twice a week, and work hard daily out of doors in all weathers, will by the time they are twenty insist on 'bettering themselves' unless they are indulged with three meals of meat daily besides their luncheon and their tea, and with as much tea, butter, sugar, and ale as they please to consume. The fault is not wholly theirs, for the example of self-indulgence has been set them by their employers . . . Far better would it be were it the habit in

Photograph of an unidentified gamekeeper with his gun and dog, circa 1895. Author's collection

English families to keep fewer servants, to pay them higher wages, and to diet them more frugally.

The fixed routine of servants' duties meant that meal times were also fixed. Breakfast was provided after the early morning chores had been completed, usually around eight o'clock. In most households, there was a short break at about eleven for 'elevenses' or what some servants called 'lunch'. The servants' main meal was dinner, served between midday and one o'clock. There would often be another short break at around four, and after the family's dinner had been served in the evening, supper was provided for servants at nine o'clock. This was usually made up of cold meat and cheese.

Although servants might expect to have some of the leftover food prepared for the family, this depended on the rules laid down by the employer. Trevor May comments that in most households, 'more expensive items were reserved for the family to eat the following day, either cold or as the basis of another dish.'

Traditionally, the cook only prepared meals for the family. According to John Robinson, a butler whose writings are quoted in John Burnett's *Useful Toil*, this left the servants 'to the tender mercies of the kitchen-maid'. He added: '. . . a huge badly cooked joint is sent to the servants' table. This appears again and again at a succession of suppers and dinners, till someone, nauseated at its continual reappearance, chops it up and assigns the greater part to the swill-tub. Any variety beyond that of a very occasional treat is out of the question.'

In households where the staff all dined together in the servants' hall, there was a strict seating order maintained, with the housekeeper at the head and the butler at the lower end of the table. The cook sat at the right of the housekeeper, and the lady's maid was on her left. The under-butler was on the right of the butler, and the coachman sat on his left. The housemaid was always next to the cook and the kitchen-maid sat by the lady's maid. The other men-servants always sat at the lower end of the table.

It was in these large households where old traditions were upheld, and the servants' dinner was eaten in silence until the end of the main course. At this point, the senior servants retired to the housekeeper's room, also known as the 'Pug's Parlour', to have their sweet (or dessert) and drink. Only after this could the junior servants relax a little.

In his memoir *Green Baize Door*, Ernest King recalled his time in service

Photograph of an unidentified cook with her kitchen staff in Sussex, 1870s. Author's collection

at the Chichester's house at Youlston Park, North Devon. Immediately after the upper servants had vacated the room,

> the babble would break out, for before [they] left we, the lesser fry, the junior footmen, the oddmen, me and the housemaids and laundry-maids would utter not a word. There was, I think, a reason for this. It instilled discipline. Had conversation been allowed from the start the meal would have been prolonged. The idea was to get it over and get back to the job. We weren't there to enjoy it. We lower servants had to walk the chalk-line.

In *From Kitchen to Garret* (1888), Mrs Panton recommended that servants in an ordinary middle-class household have 'good bread and butter, oatmeal porridge, and tea, coffee or cocoa for breakfast'. She advocated that the kitchen dinner should be the same as the dining-room luncheon but that tea might be supplemented 'by jam or an occasional home-made cake'. In Mrs

Panton's opinion, supper should be bread and cheese or soup 'made from odds and ends left at the late dinner . . . if you can trust your cook.'

If the cook could not be trusted, Mrs Panton advised laying down 'a hard and fast rule of bread and cheese' and insisting on it being kept. She gave the example of a friend who had not been so insistent. She 'went into her larder after an enormous dinner-party, expecting to find herself free from the necessity of ordering more food for at least a week, and discovered it empty . . . because, the cook informed her, they always had for their suppers any little thing "as was" left over.'

By 1911, *Cassell's Household Guide* advised that in the average middle-class household, the servant should have the same food as the rest of the family: 'This is much easier to arrange, and if the little maid is encouraged to think out and plan new ways of making and serving dishes she will delight in doing this, and very soon will be quite economical and thoughtful.'

'*Mrs Frummage's Birthday Dinner-Party*', Punch, *19 May 1866*

MRS. FRUMMAGE'S BIRTHDAY DINNER-PARTY.

Mrs. F. ("*coming from behind the Screen, sneakin' just like her*"). "THERE! OH YOU GOODFORNOTHING BOY, NOW I'VE FOUND YOU OUT. HOW DARE YOU TOUCH THE WINE, SIR!"

Robert. "PLEASE 'M, I WAS—I WAS ONLY JUST A GOIN' TO WISH YOURS AN' MASTER'S WERY GOOD 'EALTH 'M!"

Alcohol

In the eighteenth century and the first half of the nineteenth, beer allowances were part of a servant's contract, and men were usually allowed twice as much as women. Some servants were only allowed beer, and not ale. Traditionally, 'keeping beers' were always stronger than ales but 'small beer' was brewed for immediate consumption and therefore had a low alcohol content compared with ale. Large households brewed their own beer, with the butler or footman taking responsibility for the brewing and dishing out of allowances.

At Thornhill near Birmingham where Anne Boulton was mistress from 1819, the footman was in charge of the brewing. He was ordered to: 'Always draw the Ale yourself & never leave the Key. When you are likely to be out at dinner or supper, the Ale for the other Servants is drawn before you go. The men have a pint the women half a pint dinner & supper'. (MS 3782/14/83/21, Birmingham Archives and Heritage Service)

If the drinking of alcohol was not strictly controlled, staff such as coachmen, cooks, butlers and footmen could quickly develop drink problems. Writing in 1825, Samuel and Sarah Adams stressed that 'It is the business of the superior servants to see that [the servants'] accommodation is comfortable and in plenty, but without extravagance, or waste and riot.'

Some households offered tea or tea money as an alternative to beer, while others did not offer it at all. When allowances for tea and sugar were given, servants could make their own drinks in the morning and evening.

Advertisement for Cadbury's Cocoa for breakfast, The Graphic, *31 July 1886*

Chapter 8

ACCOMMODATION AND CLOTHING

Accommodation

In terms of living quarters, conditions were generally better for servants in country houses than in smaller households in towns. Landed estates usually had specific wings of the main house devoted to the 'domestic offices', including separate sleeping quarters for male and female servants, often in the attics, usually with separate staircases and entrances.

Although country house servants may have had to share rooms, they more often than not had a bed to themselves. As Pamela Sambrook points out in *Keeping Their Place*, this would have been a luxury 'after an overcrowded home'. She also asserts that 'many inventories show that it was usual to provide indoor servants with a feather bed on top of a wool mattress'.

However, the majority of male servants such as under-butlers, footmen or steward's room boys, whose job it was to guard the plate-room or the safe, were required to sleep downstairs in the basement on a fold-down bed.

The *Pall Mall Gazette* (15 January 1894) quoted the complaint of one servant who was on the committee of the London and Provincial Domestic Servants' Union:

> In most fashionable houses, footmen have to sleep on the pot-board below the kitchen-dresser, while I myself, in a former place near Hyde Park, had to sleep in a pantry, with the dustbin just outside my window, and a sink connected with a drain outside within nose-range. This meant keeping the window shut; and, considering the gas had been alight all day, you can imagine the condition of the atmosphere.

In smaller households in towns, there were often no attic rooms available for the servants' accommodation. This meant the servant had to sleep in the basement kitchen, in the same place in which she worked, giving little respite from her chores. This was the case at the home of Thomas and Jane Carlyle

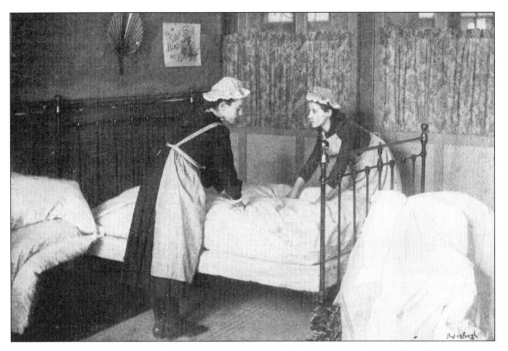

'Making a Bed: Housewifery Lessons under the London School Board', The Illustrated London News, *4 March 1893*

who lived in Cheyne Row, London from 1834. The couple were childless and had just one servant for many years. According to Judith Flanders in *The Victorian House*, a 'procession of servants slept in the back kitchen, or scullery' until 1865 when 'an additional bedroom was incorporated in the attic.'

Mrs Layton's memories of domestic service are told in *Life As We Have Known It*. She went to her first place in Hampstead at the age of 13: 'I had a very kind mistress and plenty of good food. I was fairly happy, but had to sleep in a basement kitchen which swarmed with black-beetles, and this made me very wretched at nights.'

In *From Kitchen to Garret* (1888), Mrs Panton recommended that 'the ceilings of all servants' rooms should be whitewashed once a year, and the walls colour-washed, unless these are papered with the washable sanitary wall-papers . . . and the floor should be bare of all covering, and should simply have dhurries laid down by each bed, and by the washing-stands &c.'

Mrs Panton added that every servant should have a separate bed and that it should be 'as comfortable as can be, without being unduly luxurious'. She advocated a chain or wooden-lath mattress arrangement with a good mattress on it, a pillow or two, and a bolster.

Although Mrs Panton suggested giving the servants keys to the locks on chests of drawers and wardrobes, rather harshly she was adamant that they should not keep their own boxes in their rooms because 'they cannot refrain somehow from hoarding all sorts of rubbish in them.' This assertion came from her personal experience of employing servants over twenty years. She had concluded that 'servants only feel happy if their rooms are allowed in some measure to resemble the homes of their youth' and 'the simpler . . . a servant's room is furnished the better.' In her opinion, a cupboard in which to hang up dresses, or a few hooks; a chest of drawers, washing-stand, bedchair and toilet-table with glass were all that were required in a servant's room.

As a kitchen-maid in the 1920s, Margaret Powell recalled in *Below Stairs* the bedroom she shared with the under-housemaid:

[It] was so tropical in the summer, and so freezing cold in the winter, that when we left the water in our wash jugs at night, a layer of ice formed on it, and we had to break that to wash in the morning. We couldn't even have a bath in comfort, all we had was a hip bath. For that we had to carry up every drop of water from the bathroom, two flights below, and carry it down to the lavatory when we wanted to empty it.

In addition to sleeping accommodation, the servants' quarters in country houses or large households usually had a butler's pantry, a housekeeper's room, a plate-room, kitchen, scullery and a servants' hall, as well as a dairy, laundry and rooms for cleaning lamps and boots.

The servants' hall was where male and female servants ate together, and was the hub of whatever social life was available. While in a country house it could be a sizeable room, in smaller households it might simply be the kitchen, or a small room off it, yet it still had the same title of the 'servant's hall'. Here, again, the attitudes of the employers towards the servants were reflected in the furnishings they provided before them.

Margaret Powell noted that in her first place the furniture for the servants was simply cast-offs from upstairs:

The only light we had in our servants' hall was one bulb with a white china shade. The floor was covered in old brown lino, with horrible misshapen wicker chairs which had once graced their conservatory and weren't even considered good enough for that now. Depressing walls that were shiny brown paint halfway up, and a most bilious green distemper for the top half, the barred windows and one table with an old cloth; that was our sitting room.

She contrasted this with the accommodation provided by a kind, considerate employer:

> . . . the servants' hall . . . was comfortably furnished and had a colour scheme to it. We had comfortable armchairs, a carpet on the floor, a standard lamp, and other small lamps around, pictures and ornaments. Things that you could tell were specially bought for us, not cast-offs . . . The whole room was welcoming, so that when you had spare time you felt you could really relax even though you were still on duty.

Postcard of a group of servants with their pet dog, inscribed 'Best love, from yours ever Molly xxxx Just a friendly group of us all, my best Pall [sic] beside me', circa 1905. Author's collection

Clothing

For a female servant, print dresses for morning work and black dresses for afternoon wear were the unofficial uniform, teamed with white caps and plain white or striped aprons. If she worked in the kitchen, the same dress was worn for the morning and afternoon. However, finding the money to pay for such clothing to start a job in service could be extremely difficult, and might mean a burden for her parents or taking a temporary job to save up for them.

Margaret Thomas was one of five children and her father died when she was 4. At the age of 14, she started looking after a baby and doing light jobs, then took a place cleaning knives and boots. In *The Day Before Yesterday*, she recalled: 'Eventually I saved enough and got my uniform: print dresses, morning aprons, black dress, afternoon aprons, stiff collars, and cuffs, all packed into a tin trunk, and set off to my first real job. I was just fifteen.'

In *Below Stairs*, Margaret Powell remembered how in the 1920s her mother had to borrow £2 to pay for the uniform her daughter needed for her first place as kitchen-maid at a large house in Hove, Sussex. She required 'three print dresses, blue or green; four white aprons with bibs, and four caps; stockings, and black strapped shoes'. As Margaret recalled, 'Apart from the uniform my own clothes were very few indeed. I was dressed up in a blouse and skirt and a coat that had belonged to my grandmother.'

Being given a dress length was a standard Christmas present for female servants, but it was usually for work, not out of hours and therefore not necessarily a pattern they would have chosen for themselves. In any case, unless they were skilled in dressmaking, they still had to find the money to have the dress made up for them. Even if they could make their own clothes, there was very little free time in which to do it. Clothing might also be given when a master or mistress died and the family went into mourning.

The wearing of caps and bonnets, and even hairstyles, was very strictly regulated, giving rise to much disagreement between employer and servant. Female servants were expected to dress modestly but not to wear clothing above their station. As Anne Boulton advised her housemaid at Thornhill in the 1820s: 'Let your dress be always neat and clean, but never fine'. (MS 3782/14/83/21, Birmingham Archives and Heritage Service)

Employers could, and did, regulate the amount of decoration and the material their servants' clothes were made from, and this extended to their off-duty hours. In the 1880s, a large number of newspaper advertisements for servants' positions started to specify 'No fringes'. This was a reference to

Morning wear for a general servant, Cassell's Household Guide, *1911*

a particular style of hair, the objection presumably being that if the servant had such a fringe, she was too busy thinking about her appearance to do her job properly. Here is an example from *The Morning Post* (8 January 1889):

> WANTED as soon as possible by Lady residing in Hampton Court Palace. Thoroughly good PARLOURMAID; wait on lady, lamps, good needlewoman. Also Thoroughly good HOUSEMAID, good needlewoman; no beer; ages 22 to 28; tall; Protestants; good recommendations necessary; no fringes; country servants preferred. Apply first by letter to Mrs H. B., Belvedere, 43 Hamilton-road, Ealing W.

In its own inimitable way, *Punch* (8 March 1884) poked fun at one particular advertisement which appeared in the *Daily Telegraph*:

> 'A Lady requires good PLAIN COOK, for small family. Good personal character necessary. Wages £18, all found but beer. No fringe. Apply this evening, five to nine.'

> Mr PUNCH, who is very particular with regard to the costume of his Parlour-maids, would not for a moment presume to interfere with his Cook. As long as his dinner is well cooked and punctuality observed, his Cook may wear a scarlet gown if she pleases, and her hair in ringlets.
>
> It is possible to imagine followers being prohibited, but we fail to understand, if the Cook derives sweet consolation from a fringe, why she should not be permitted to indulge therein. Fancy, if this Lady compels the Cook she engages to abolish her fringe, what revenge may follow. There is no member of a household so capable of making everyone of the family so miserable as the Cook, if she gives her mind to it . . . It is plain that the above-mentioned Advertiser considers a good plain Cook cannot be too plain.

In *Life As We Have Known It*, Mrs Layton commented on some very specific conditions to which she had to agree on accepting a place in the 1870s with a lady and her daughter:

> First, I was to take the pads out of my hair (large chignons being then the fashion); second, I was to cut the tail off my dress (long dresses were then worn); third, I was to wear aprons with bibs to them (which were never worn in those days). All three I objected to, but I

finally agreed to cut off the tail on my dress and to put bibs to my aprons, but I would not take my hair down.

When it came to clothing, footmen and coachmen had a distinct advantage over female servants since liveries were provided for them. These were elaborate dress uniforms that, as Pamela Sambrook points out in *Keeping Their Place*, were 'a deliberate throwback to an earlier fashion, marking the servant out as not a gentleman but belonging to one ... A sign of status and conspicuous consumption for the employer, livery was the opposite for the wearer.'

According to Mrs Beeton in her *Book of Household Management*, the footman only had to provide his own stockings, shoes and washing:

Where silk stockings, or other extra articles of linen are worn, they are found by the family, as well as his livery, a working dress, consisting of a pair of overalls, a waistcoat, a fustian jacket, with a white or jean one for times when he is liable to be called to answer the door or wait at breakfast; and, on quitting his service, he is expected to leave behind him any livery had within six months.

Chapter 9

HEALTHCARE AND OLD AGE

Healthcare

The sheer quantity of physical work expected of domestic servants frequently led to bouts of illness. This was less of a problem for servants working for the landed gentry as they could expect to be looked after whenever they were ill. According to Pamela Sambrook in *Keeping Their Place*, the Dunham Massey estate had a 'long tradition of patriarchal care for its employees'. She comments that in 1822 more money was spent on medical bills for the servants than the family 'despite the fact that the family members were treated by an expensive doctor, while the servants were prescribed for by an apothecary from Altrincham'.

Employers were often subscribers to the local general hospital, which entitled them to recommend a set number of people per year for medical treatment. Although they were expected to pay for their own servants' treatment, they could legitimately recommend the families of their servants.

Those working in domestic service in smaller households were not so well looked after. In *Yes, Ma'am! Glimpses of Domestic Service 1901–1951*, M C Scott-Moncrieff quotes from the memories of Isabella (Bella) Anderson as she goes to her second position:

> I was at it from early morning till late at night, and I did not get out till after three on a Sunday, in at nine, and never to church. This lady had a lot of dinner parties, twelve or fourteen sitting at the table. My food was nothing like the food I had in the first place. By the end of six months, I was ill. The day I left, I went straight to the family doctor in St Andrews. He phoned for a bed in the Cottage Hospital and I was in three weeks with very bad anaemia, and fluid on the knee. I was off work for two months and unfit for quite a while.

Many illnesses suffered by servants were directly related to the occupation itself. *Household Words* (24 August 1850), edited by Charles Dickens, quoted the case of a poor servant girl afflicted with 'a disease to which the domestics

'Helping Gardener', drawn by Robert Barnes, The Graphic, *26 July 1890*

of the middle classes, especially, are very liable – white swelling of the knee'. When she presented herself at a hospital, she was told that an operation would be 'certain death' and therefore she was incurable, and could not be admitted. With no relations to call on for help, the girl '[crawled] back to a miserable lodging, she lay helpless till her small savings were exhausted. Privations of the severest kind followed; and despite the assistance of some benevolent persons who learnt her condition when it was too late, she died a painful and wretched death.' Charles Dickens called this situation 'a marvellous oversight of benevolence'.

Old Age

On retirement, some long-serving members of staff in country houses were rewarded with a pension or annuity, or accommodation in an estate cottage or almshouse. However, these were the lucky ones. As Pamela Sambrook points out in *Keeping Their Place*, 'country-house servants were well paid and expected to save for their old age.'

The very nature of domestic service meant that retired servants had no place of their own. What could an elderly servant do if he or she was too ill to work, and had not been able to save for retirement? One option was to approach the former employer for help, but all too often these appeals fell on deaf ears, especially if a number of years had passed since leaving service.

The majority of retired servants had no wealthy employer to appeal to and, sadly, they were destined to end their days in the workhouse. In 1846, the Domestic Servants' Benevolent Institution was founded as a direct response to the large numbers of destitute elderly servants who became workhouse inmates in their final years.

The situation was particularly bad in London where the workhouse wards were full of ex-servants. According to Pamela Horn in *The Rise and Fall of the Victorian Servant*, in 1871 at Kensington Poor Law Infirmary 'fifty-five of the 130 female inmates recorded in the census were domestic servants; and at St George's Workhouse, Hanover Square, there were 133 female domestic servants out of a total of 434 female inmates.'

The problem was not confined to female servants either. As Eric Horne pointed out in *What The Butler Winked At*, 'Perhaps one in a hundred butlers gets a sort of pension, enough to keep him out of the workhouse.' He added:

> If a man has a family and wife to keep, and house rent to pay, there is not much left out of a wage of seventy or eighty pounds a year, finding his own clothes. If a servant is an honest man and has to do the above, he will be worse off at the end of thirty years' service than when he began. He may, if he is a single man all his life, manage to keep out of the workhouse at the end, but he would have to be lucky, and have found good situations . . .

It was not until the twentieth century that government legislation offered some form of security for domestic servants in the form of the Old Age Pensions Act (1908) and the National Insurance Bill (1911).

Part 3

ROLES OF SERVANTS

Chapter 10

MALE SERVANTS

The Butler

Butlers were usually employed in larger households, where they were in charge of the male servants, specifically the footman or footmen whom they directed. The butler had two main responsibilities: the plate chest and the wine cellar. Every night, he had to make sure the everyday plate was put away carefully, and it was he who handed it out for cleaning every morning. He was also in charge of the plate used for special occasions such as balls or dinner parties.

The title of butler comes from the Old French word 'bouteillier', which means a servant who looked after the bottles and casks. Overseeing the wine cellars, decanting the wine and managing the brewing process (if it was carried out on the premises) formed a major part of his role.

It was the butler's task to keep a cellar book and to enter into it daily the amount of wine given out, and the number of bottles drunk. According to *The Servants' Practical Guide* (1880), the cellar book was 'the check upon the butler as to the quantity of wine drunk in a given time'. The butler also had to decant the wine each day.

Given this experience, it is perhaps unsurprising that many ex-butlers chose to run public houses or other forms of hospitality when they left domestic service. James Brown, the butler of Lord Byron, went on to found the famous Mayfair hotel bearing his name in 1837, along with his wife Sarah, who had been Lady Byron's lady's maid.

The personal appearance of male servants, particularly butlers and footmen, was of utmost consideration for employers when making a new appointment. Any blemishes or imperfections, especially the ravages of smallpox, might have a detrimental impact on whether a man was offered a post or not.

In *Keeping Their Place*, Pamela Sambrook comments that in 1819 John Trevanion, a friend of the sixth Earl of Stamford, secured the services of a butler for the earl's new household at Dunham Massey. He wrote: 'I have engaged Philip Osgood at 70 gs [guineas] per annum for you without any perquisites, if his character answers . . . Philip Osgood is <u>rather</u> marked with the small pox and a little freckled but is in my opinion certainly a respectable & genteel looking servant.' In this instance, Philip Osgood's scars did not prevent him from obtaining the post and he 'remained a kingpin of the Earl's household for many years.'

The butler did not wear livery, which was an indication of his higher status, and he had to provide his own clothing and pay for his washing. In *The Complete Servant*, Samuel and Sarah Adams noted that he was 'expected to be genteel and clean in his person' at all times.

His domain was the butler's pantry, where the silver was kept in a special plate chest or other cabinet that could be locked. Larger houses had a separate plate-room where the silver was cleaned by the footman. The glass was also kept in the pantry along with the china; although in some places the china was stored in the housekeeper's room. A wooden sink in the pantry would have been used to wash up the glass and/or china, but again this was the footman's job. The butler's bedroom was usually close to his pantry.

If no valet was kept, the duty of dressing his master and looking after his clothes fell to the butler. The nature of the butler's remaining duties depended on how many footmen were on the staff. If two or three were kept, the butler waited at table during breakfast, luncheon, tea and supper, supervising the arrangements for each meal and pouring the wine. In the afternoon, he had to be ready to announce visitors, and at all times had to make sure that the drawing-room, morning-room and library were ready for use. This might include rearranging books; cutting, airing and folding newspapers; or putting blinds up or down.

Preparing the daily newspaper was a skilled job. It was delivered wet, in one large sheet and each page had to be cut, folded and ironed to remove the damp. According to Edward Hayward in *Upstairs and Downstairs: Life in an English Country House*, 'a really professional steward or butler would then stitch them together.'

Where only one footman was kept, the butler had to assist him in much of the pantry work, including laying the table, waiting and clearing away at breakfast and luncheon, cleaning the plate and attending to the lamps. When the footman was out on carriage duty in the afternoon, the butler attended to the fires in the various downstairs reception rooms and prepared the five o'clock tea in time for his mistress's return.

Samuel and Sarah Adams were unanimous in their view that the butler was essential to a well-run household:

Postcard of an unidentified footman, circa 1905. Author's collection

In all things connected with the establishment, he is supposed, when no steward is kept, to represent his master; and as various accounts are under his direction, he ought to be able to write a fair hand, and to be ready in the first rules of arithmetic . . . a Butler who knows his duties, and performs them with zeal, integrity, and ability, cannot be too highly prized by judicious heads of families.

As an upper servant with a great deal of responsibility, it was difficult for butlers to have personal relationships. In his memoir *What the Butler Winked At*, Eric Horne commented:

Taking all things into consideration, a butler ought not to be married. It is not fair to the wife, for she has to mope at home, seeing very little of her husband, while he is at the big house, surrounded with all sorts of womenfolk . . . Should he happen to beget several children, it all goes against them, for the children must not be seen about the place.

Ignoring his own advice, Eric Horne did get married but ended up living apart from his wife and children because his 'rotter' of a first position as butler 'sickened' her of domestic service.

The Under-Butler

Large country houses often employed an under-butler, who worked under the direction of the butler: cleaning the plate and the parlour knives and forks; laying the cloths; setting out the sideboard; trimming the dining-room and drawing-room lamps; helping the butler to clean his master's clothes and shoes; and assisting to wait at table. After dinner, he was expected to clean the plate in the butler's pantry so he did not have to answer any bells during that period. Unlike footmen, there was no specified height for under-butlers because they were not on show to guests until dinner.

John Bennet, Butler

Born in around 1761, John Bennet's early life and his place of birth is a mystery. He married Sophia Noxon in June 1801 at St Marylebone, London and his first child Elizabeth Drury Bennet was born the following April in Chipping Camden, Gloucestershire. This was also Sophia's place of birth.

In November 1803, the couple's second child was born in Himley,

Staffordshire. John's earlier occupation is not known but it is safe to assume he had previously worked in domestic service because he was to become butler to William, Lord Viscount Dudley and Ward whose seat was at Himley Hall.

Being appointed a butler to the nobility would only have been possible if he had previous experience in a similar occupation, preferably in a large household, with an exemplary character reference. As John was in his forties in the 1800s, he would have had plenty of time to establish such a career, perhaps working his way up from boot-boy, under-footman, footman, under-butler and then butler.

It is not clear when he was appointed in his role as butler, but the first reference to John working at Himley Hall appears in August 1811 in the estate's casual payments book for 1796–1817. John was paid £25 for 'Servants travelling Exp. to London'. As a butler, John was in a trustworthy role handling large sums of money, and it appears he was responsible for paying for the servants' coaching expenses between Himley and London. (DE/IV/10/1 Ledgers 1796–1817 Casual Payments, Dudley Archives and Local History Service)

The period between April and August was the London season when the landed gentry decamped to the capital for five months of socialising. The Dudley family's London residence was at Dudley House, Park Lane. Although many of the staff would have stayed at Himley Hall to undertake spring cleaning and housekeeping duties, as butler, John would have gone with his master. There is no record of Lord Dudley having a valet, so it is likely that John was also fulfilling this role.

There are similar reimbursements to John and to William Webb (the coachman), usually in April and August, until August 1822, although the accounts book continues until May 1823.

It is believed that John's wife Sophia and his five children were living in a cottage on the Himley estate. If John was away from Himley for five months of the year, this may have put a strain on family relationships.

Other reimbursements listed in the casual payments book while John was in Himley, rather than London, include two payments of £5 5s in November and December 1814 for paying 'Dr Johnson's Fee [to] attend E Hitchcock'. Eliza Hitchcock was one of the housemaids at Himley Hall.

Although wages books exist for the period in which John was working at Himley Hall, they only list female indoor staff such as the housekeeper, housemaids and kitchen-maids, and male outdoor staff including the gardener, a number of grooms and the brewer.

Unusually, they do not mention John, the coachman William Webb or any other male indoor staff, nor a lady's maid for Lord Dudley's wife, Julia, Viscountess Dudley and Ward (and such a maid would undoubtedly have been employed). One explanation for this could be that there was a separate accounts book in the Himley Hall estate records for paying these salaries which has not survived, or a separate book was kept at Dudley House in London.

Whatever the reason, the records do not reveal the amount of John's salary.

In Samuel and Sarah Adams's book *The Complete Servant*, written in 1825, it was noted that 'the wages of regular butlers, in large families, are from £50 to £80 per annum' but it is possible that John was receiving a higher salary than this, given that he was working for the nobility.

There is, however, one reference to him receiving £50 as 'half a year annuity' on 29 September 1832. (DE/IV/10/3 Dudley Estates Copy of Downing's Cash Account 1832, 1 volume, copied 1848, Dudley Archives and Local History Service)

William, Lord Viscount Dudley and Ward died on 5 May 1823 without leaving a will. His son and heir, John William, Earl of Dudley, would have had his own butler so it is probable that John Bennet retired from working for the Dudley family shortly after his master died. When his seventh child, Maria, was christened at Himley in August 1824, John was described as 'late Butler to Lord Dudley'. Although Lord Dudley died intestate, it is highly likely that it was his son who sanctioned the annuity for John, as recognition of his long years of service for his father. The payment of this annuity would have ceased upon his death.

John Bennet had seven children with his wife Sophia, although the third child, John, died aged 7 in 1813. Sophia died in April 1836 aged 57. Despite having six children to provide for, John Bennet was able to amass a considerable fortune for the time, and to raise his status in society. In the 1834 *White's Gazetteer and Directory* for Staffordshire, he was described as a 'gentleman' in the list of private residents in

Himley, and when he died in April 1839 he was able to leave his children some substantial legacies in his will:

I bequeath . . . to my Daughter Eliza Two Hundred and Fifty Pounds, To my Son George and also to my Son John each of them Two Hundred and Fifty Pounds, To my Daughter Mary Five Hundred Pounds, To my Daughter Sophia One Thousand Pounds, and To my Daughter Maria Six Hundred Pounds, whatever there may be remaining when all the Legacies and my Debts are paid to be equally divided amongst my six Children share and share alike . . .

The value of his estate was sworn at under £4,000.

(With thanks to Carolyn Middleton for this information about her ancestor.)

The House Steward

According to Pamela Sambrook in *Keeping Their Place*, becoming a house steward was 'the highest achievement for an indoor manservant'. He was head of all the family households 'and responsible for a myriad of mundane duties'.

In *The Complete Servant*, Samuel and Sarah Adams commented that the house steward was 'the most important officer in domestic establishments' but was only employed in families of great fortunes 'to superintend such necessary business . . . they cannot undertake, but also to control and manage . . . all the most important concerns of the household.' His chief business was 'to hire, manage, and direct, and discharge every servant of every denomination.' Book-keeping was a major part of his job, and where there was a steward, it was he who paid all the tradesmen's bills and the servants' salaries. As such, his character needed to be 'irreproachable and exemplary, that he may be regarded with confidence and satisfaction by his employers, and respected by those around him'.

The Steward's Room Boy

A steward's room boy was appointed to assist the steward in running errands, carrying messages, waiting at table in the steward's room, trimming the lamps below stairs and cleaning the servants' boots and shoes.

The Valet

A valet was the male equivalent of the lady's maid, being the personal assistant of his master. *The Servants' Practical Guide* (1880) noted that valets were 'generally kept by single . . . and elderly gentlemen, and seldom by married men'.

According to Samuel and Sarah Adams, the valet's duties were 'not so various nor so important as those of the footman' and were frequently, especially in small families, a part of the business of a footman. The valet was not a liveried servant and therefore did not receive a clothing allowance, although his master's cast-off clothes were usually given to him as perquisites. In *Upstairs and Downstairs: Life in an English Country House*, Edward Hayward comments that 'A good valet's experience and panache had to be recognised with excellent wages and a high level of trust.' Tips and presents were a regular addition to his salary.

In his memoir *What the Butler Winked At*, Eric Horne recalls how, in the 1890s, he was paid £100 a year as valet to an employer he called Sir Cayenne, famed for swearing. Many valets were able to earn enough to set up as hoteliers or shop-keepers.

The valet's duties revolved around helping his master to dress and undress, and attending to his master's clothing and personal appearance. This might include carrying up the water for his master's bath; cleaning shooting, walking and dress boots as well as top-boots; shaving his master if required; waiting upon his master at meals; and packing and unpacking clothes when travelling.

According to Edward Hayward, the valet 'travelled everywhere of conse-quence with his master, deciphering train timetables and taking charge of valuables and cash', and acting as a courier and interpreter when abroad. When visiting valets stayed at a country house with their masters, they were often asked to help the butler wait at dinner if there was a large party, although this was not a popular part of the job.

A valet to an elderly gentleman would also be expected to help with regards to his master's health, including sitting up late, carrying him up and down stairs during the day, or sleeping in his room at night. As such, he was expected to be physically fit.

In *The Complete Servant*, Samuel and Sarah Adams warned:

As the valet is much about his master's person, and has the opportunity of hearing his off-at-hand opinions on many subjects, he should endeavour to have as short a memory as possible, and, above all, keep his master's council; and he should be very cautious of mischief-making or tale-bearing, to the prejudice of other persons, as calculated to involve his master in disputes, and ruin himself, if by chance he is incorrect.

The Man-Cook

In grand houses, the cook was often a man because his appointment was a symbol of his employer's prestige. The wealthiest households employed a French chef or even an Italian confectioner.

According to Samuel and Sarah Adams, the 'man Cook . . . is generally a foreigner, or if an Englishman, possesses a peculiar tact in manufacturing many fashionable foreign delicacies, or of introducing certain seasonings and flavours in his dishes, which render them more inviting to the palate of his employer, than those produced by the simple healthy modes of modern English Cooks.'

The man-cook superintended the kitchen while his female assistants were charged with roasting, boiling and the ordinary work of the kitchen. His attention was 'chiefly directed to the stew-pan, in the manufacture of stews, fracassees, fricandeaux &c'. His situation was one of great labour and fatigue with 'superior skill requisite for excellence in his art', and because of this, he was able to command a salary two or three times higher than that given to the most experienced female cook. Samuel and Sarah Adams noted that HRH the Duke of York paid Monsieur Ude, his French cook, £500 per annum.

They considered a man-cook to be 'economical because he produces an inexhaustible variety without any waste of materials'. In 1825, when the Adamses wrote *A Complete Servant*, they estimated that only 300 or 400 wealthy families kept men-cooks, and they were also employed in forty or fifty London hotels. They added: 'it is usual in smaller establishments to engage a man-cook for a day or two before an entertainment.'

The Footman

The duties of the footman were deemed by Samuel and Sarah Adams to be 'multifarious and incessant', making him the lynchpin of a large household. Before the family's breakfast, there was the cleaning of the plate and all of the boots to be done, as well as carrying coals to the sitting-room and trimming all the lamps. Footmen had to wait at breakfast, luncheon, tea and dinner, laying the table for those meals and clearing away, plus washing any china, glass or silver used.

Postcard of an unidentified groom with horse, circa 1900. Author's collection

It was also the footman's duty to deliver messages and answer the door to visitors, and it was he who went out with the carriage in the afternoon, and again in the evening if required. In addition, the footman had to attend to the fires in the sitting-rooms throughout the day and evening, and to light the house at dusk, whether with gas, lamps or candles. He was also expected to act as valet to the young gentlemen of the house. During meals, his place was behind his master's chair.

In her *Book of Household Management*, Mrs Beeton stressed that footmen should be 'attentive to all . . . [and] obtrusive to none', especially when attending in the dining-room and the drawing-room. They were advised to move about 'actively but noiselessly' with 'no creaking of shoes, which is an abomination . . .'

Despite this seemingly never-ending list of tasks, much of what footmen did in large households was 'close waiting'. This meant being available to carry out tasks for the family such as serving meals or delivering messages, or as Pamela Sambrook puts it 'waiting to be needed'. In *Keeping Their Place*, she explains a rota system which many large households used:'. . . if a house had three footmen, each one would be in close waiting one day out of three, carriage duty on the second day and the third would be a day off waiting, with only the normal duties of the pantry, meals and valeting.'

An indication of the varied nature of errands a footman might have to make can be gleaned from an account book for Rufford Hall, the seat of Sir Thomas George Hesketh. Covering the period 1877–82, the book includes entries for the expenses of the footman Henry Duffell, for which he was reimbursed by the land agent, Thomas Ogilvy. His errands included 'taking Miss Hesketh's Dog to Preston', going 'to Easton & back with Pictures' and travelling 'to & from London with Sir Thomas'. Easton was the Hesketh family's other residence in Northamptonshire. (DDHE 62/140 Personal Account Book 1877–1882, Lancashire Archives)

In small families where he was the only man-servant, the footman's main duties were to clean the knives, shoes, plate and furniture; answer the door, go on errands, wait at table and answer the parlour bell. From the mid-nineteenth century, knife-cleaning machines could be used to lighten the load.

Footmen were required to have a handsome appearance and in job advertisements specified heights were requested as employers liked their footmen to 'match up' if they had more than one. A height of six feet or more was preferred; livery uniforms were passed on to replacement footmen.

The height of a footman could also affect his pay. In *The Victorian Domestic Servant*, Trevor May comments that 'at the end of the nineteenth century, £20–£22 a year was the going rate in London for a footman measuring 5 feet 6 inches. At 6 feet he might have expected £32–£40.' A good pair of calves was also 'an important requisite', since the footman's breeches and silk stockings put them on show.

As a liveried servant, a footman was usually allowed two suits of livery each year. Livery was an extremely elaborate uniform designed to show off the master's wealth and social status, and the footman would wear his best livery when going out with the carriage. His livery usually consisted of dress suits and undress suits, several hats and pairs of boots, a great coat and separate clothing for morning work.

Samuel and Sarah Adams advised the footman to complete the dirtiest part of his work first, during which time 'his working dress should generally be a pair of overalls, a waistcoat and fustian jacket, and a leather apron, with a white apron to put on occasionally, when called from these duties.' They also stressed that when the carriage waited for his employer at public places, the footman 'should abstain from drinking with other servants, and take care to be within call when wanted.'

Christopher Latimer, Footman

Born in Stanwix, Carlisle in 1830, Christopher Latimer was listed as a footman on the 1851 census at Eden Hall in Cumberland, the country seat of Sir George Musgrave. In this employment, he was paid a salary of £25 4s per year. It is not known when he arrived at Eden Hall or for how long he stayed, but unlike some of his colleagues, he did not make a career out of being in service.

This may have had something to do with the fact he got married just two years later. Although it was not unheard of for footmen to be married and to have their wife and family ensconced in a cottage nearby, this scenario was not always conducive to a happy family life. Employers preferred their servants to be without encumbrances or dependants, and like other domestic staff, footmen were expected to be at the beck and call of their masters and mistresses. It is likely that Christopher would have felt torn between his employer and his new 'encumbrance', his wife Elizabeth.

By the time of the 1861 census, he and his wife, together with their 6-year-old daughter, were living in Caldewgate, Cumberland. He was listed as 'servant waiter', a job more suited to family life. Ten years later, Christopher was an innkeeper at the White Horse Inn in Carlisle.

In large households, footmen were often called 'John', 'William', 'Henry' or 'Thomas', regardless of their real names, presumably so that employers did not have to remember new names when their footmen left and were replaced.

Where two or more footmen were kept, the under-footman carried out the duties which were 'deemed the most laborious' – for instance, cleaning knives and forks, boots and shoes, carrying up coals and attending all the fires above stairs during the day. He also carried cards and messages, and helped to carry up and wait at dinner.

In *What the Butler Winked At*, Eric Horne recalled how, in the 1860s, he discovered what real gentleman's service was when he obtained a place as second footman ('being a tall boy for my age') to a baronet about forty miles from his home:

It was a good, old-fashioned country place: hunting, shooting, fishing was indulged in. The first footman and I had sixty-three colza oil lamps to clean and trim, before breakfast, after collecting them from all parts of the house. About twenty servants were kept. The butler taught me how to polish silver properly, and all my other duties . . . After supper we had dancing in the servants' hall.

Sadly, after about two years, the baroness died and the household staff was reduced, leaving Eric looking for another job.

The Page or Hall-Boy

The most junior indoor male servant was a page or hall-boy, and he was usually only employed in large households or country houses. He ran errands, cleaned boots, fetched coal and answered doors. If he was employed as a page, he might have a liveried uniform. Before starting in service, the page or hall-boy needed money for shoes, shirts and stiff collars, which could be a real drain on his parents' finances. However, from this position, he could work his way up to footman, under-butler and perhaps butler.

Wages receipt for Robert Waller, coachman at Eden Hall, Cumbria, 11 November 1868. Author's collection

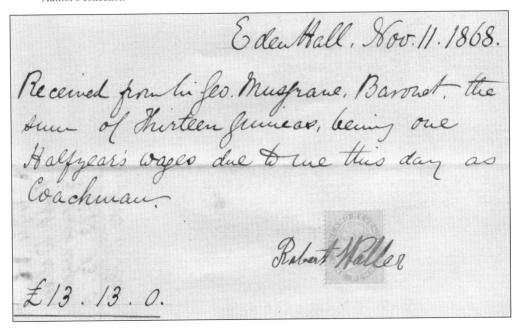

The Coachman

The main duty of the coachman was to drive the carriage skilfully and safely because, in Mrs Beeton's words, 'much of the enjoyment of those in the carriage depends on his proficiency in his art – much also of the wear of the carriage and horses.' She stressed that he should know 'the pace at which he can go over the road he has under him, without risking the springs, and without shaking those he is driving too much'. A moderate pace was seven or eight miles an hour.

For Samuel and Sarah Adams, it was vital that the coachman should take 'care in driving his horses so as to preserve his own family and not injure other passengers on horse or foot, that he may not involve his master in law-suits, and wound the feelings of those he is driving, is of the utmost consequence'. They added: 'On the sobriety, steady conduct and respectable appearance of this important servant, depend the exterior appearance of the family with which he resides.' This was because his employers' friends, family and acquaintances saw the coachman every time they visited or the master and mistress paid them a call.

He had to work long hours, especially if his employer did a great deal of socialising, as he had to wait until they were finished dining at other houses or attending functions before he could bring them home.

In addition to his driving duties, the coachman needed a good general knowledge of horses as he often had to assist his employer when purchasing new ones. It was his responsibility to oversee the stables and to make sure the horses were regularly fed, properly groomed and that minor ailments were quickly treated. Maintaining and cleaning the carriage was also an important duty.

The coachman's daily routine depended upon how many additional servants were kept to work in the stables, and whether there was more than one coachman. If only one coachman was employed, his duties included the whole of the stable work, as well as cleaning, greasing and examining the carriage. Before breakfast, he and the groom took care of the horses. The most recently used harnesses were also meticulously cleaned. After eating, they put the stables in good order, in readiness for a visit from their master who would give the orders for the day. Otherwise, the coachman would attend his master and mistress for orders later in the morning.

The coachman's morning tasks continued with the cleaning of the coach or coaches. This was a lengthy but necessary job which included washing the carriage parts and wheels with water, blacking the straps and all other parts made of leather, greasing or oiling the bed of the carriage, and firmly securing the lynchpins. The inside of the carriage was then brushed, the glasses cleaned, and the lamps cleaned and trimmed.

Like footmen, the coachman was a liveried servant and he had to dress himself just before the time the coach was ordered, in order to keep his livery clean. After returning in the afternoon, or the evening if he had to go out again, the coachman had to wash and clean his coach 'if there be time and daylight', otherwise it was left until the morning.

What could not be left was the care of the horses, and before he could retire for the night, the coachman had to make sure the regular stable duties were attended to, and that his horses were watered, fed, rubbed down, littered and racked up as usual. If he did not have to go out with the coach in the evening, this was done at eight o'clock.

According to Samuel and Sarah Adams, if an under-coachman was kept, 'he attends with the assistance of the helper, to the care and dressing of his horses, washing and cleaning the harness and coach, which is always the second best, and is driven by him at night; whereas the best coach and the best horses are driven by the head coachman by day.' The under-coachman was sometimes required to ride as postillion, or as courier, when the family travelled post. For this method of transport, the family used their own carriage but fresh horses were supplied at each stopping place.

At Thornhill, the home of Anne Boulton, the coachman had a number of different duties. He was required to take charge of the carriage and two horses, as well as the pigs and poultry, and to clean out their sties and yards every morning. The stable, manger and saddle house had to be thoroughly cleaned out once a week, and the carriage was cleaned before breakfast every day 'except on mowing mornings'. The coachman was also expected to 'occasionally pump water, fill the Coal hole, help to shake Carpets, wait at Table when required, assist in the brewing, wheel the Garden Chair . . .' He was to make sure that no servants sat in the saddle house and that fires were put out before dark. To top it off, if he wanted to go out, he had to ask leave and 'be at home by nine o'clock'. (MS 3782/14/83/21 Birmingham Archives and Heritage Service)

Robert Waller, Coachman

Born in Bedford, Bedfordshire in around 1820, Robert Waller was to spend more than thirty years working for the Musgrave family who owned the Eden Hall estate in Cumberland. Robert is recorded as working as a groom there from at least November 1838 when he signed a wages receipt for £9 10s for half a year.

Robert married Elizabeth Graham in 1843 and settled in a cottage on the estate. On the 1851 census, he was still recorded as a groom and he had four children. By 1861, he had been promoted to coachman and in 1868 his wages were £13 13s for half a year. This was a considerable increase on his pay as a groom.

It is not clear when Robert left Eden Hall as coachman but by 1881 he was a 'retired coachman' and was living in Edenhall village. No further information can be obtained about him from the censuses.

The Groom

The groom had to rise extremely early in the morning, about 5 am in the summer and 6 am in the winter, as did everyone else working in the stables. If he had two or more horses to look after, with a chaise or other vehicle, he usually had a boy to help him in the stable. Every groom fed his own horses and dressed them, brushing and examining them carefully.

If the groom's master was in the habit of riding out in the morning before breakfast, he had to rise much earlier to get the horses ready for himself and his master. Every time they returned from a ride or from pulling a carriage or gig, the horses were attended to first before the harness and vehicle. At around eight o'clock in the evening, the groom did his final round of the stables: cleaning it out; feeding, watering and rubbing down the horses; littering them up, bandaging their legs (to prevent swelling) and stopping their feet (if heated); and racking them up for the night.

A groom often had close contact with the younger members of the family, perhaps teaching them to ride on a pony and helping them to improve their riding skills. In *Late Victorian Britain*, J F C Harrison quotes from the memoirs of Siegfried Sassoon, who was born in 1886. He had a particular fondness for his aunt's groom with whom he spent a lot of time during his childhood: 'He was what I afterwards learnt to call "a perfect gentleman's servant", he never allowed me to forget my position as "a little gentleman": he always

Postcard of an unidentified coachman with whip, circa 1900. Author's collection

knew exactly when to become discreetly respectful. In fact, he "knew his place."'

The Stable-Boy

A stable-boy was a young lad who helped the coachman and groom in cleaning out the stables, the horses, the harness and carriages, and assisting with anything else which needed doing. This was another junior male servant position, which a boy might take if he knew he preferred being out of doors to serving in the 'big house'. A boy could progress from this position to groom, and perhaps coachman in later years.

The Chauffeur

In the late nineteenth and early twentieth century, when motor cars started to be used by the gentry, chauffeurs were needed to drive them around. For coachmen, trained only in the art of driving carriages and used only to horses, this usually meant having to find new employment, unless they were prepared to learn to drive. However, most were suspicious of the new vehicles, and as a result, many of the first chauffeurs were French or German, because they were trained at the factories in which the cars were built. In *Upstairs and Downstairs: Life in an English Country House*, Edward Hayward comments that 'as newcomers and foreigners, they were rarely popular with the other servants.'

According to Eric Horne in *What the Butler Winked At*, these new chauffeurs were a completely different class of servant:

> When motors were first used, a lot of men learnt to drive that knew nothing of the working of a gentleman's house, and in most cases the old coachman had either to learn to drive, or get the sack. These new class of men would come into the house, smoke cigarettes, throw ends of cigarettes and burnt matches all over the place.

Like footmen and coachmen, chauffeurs wore a smart uniform when they were working. In the 1920s, Margaret Powell was a kitchen-maid in a large London house. In *Below Stairs*, she recalled the excitement associated with dinner parties because the chauffeurs who brought the guests sat in the servants' hall while their employers were upstairs:

> You never saw such a fluttering in the dovecote as there used to be on these occasions. There we were, six or seven of us women who hardly ever spoke to a man . . . Our servants' hall would be a sort of

magnet for the females, even the sewing-maid and the nurse-maid would find some excuse or other to come down. And all because of these chauffeurs in their uniforms.

The Gardener

According to Samuel and Sarah Adams in *The Complete Servant*, a head gardener in charge of managing a gentleman's garden and grounds had to be:

perfect in the ordinary business, and the regular routine of digging, cropping, and managing a kitchen garden, but also . . . well versed in the nature of soils, manures, and composts, the best methods of propagating plants, shrubs, and trees, the management of the hothouse, greenhouse, conservatory, hotbeds; and the culture, not only of indigenous, but also of foreign and exotic productions.

Not surprisingly, given this long list of skills and attributes required, the position was relatively well paid. In 1825, it was anything from £50 to £100 a year with a cottage in the grounds, and vegetables and fuel usually allowed. At Himley Hall in Staffordshire, the gardener, Stephen Drewett, was paid £52 10s a year in the 1820s. (DE/IV10/2 Ledgers 1817–1823, Dudley Archives and Local History Service)

On large country estates, most produce was home-grown and in *Upstairs and Downstairs: Life in an English Country House*, Edward Hayward comments that 'an immaculate garden full of exotic plants and furniture was considered a mark of the family's prestige and civilization.' He adds that some head gardeners, like Joseph Paxton at Chatsworth, 'had an international reputation for some plant discovery' and were paid 'at the very highest rate for servants'.

Under-gardeners worked under the direction of the head gardener, usually in 'digging, trenching, wheeling, dunging, gravelling, hoeing, mowing and other laborious work'. They were paid on a weekly basis, and some under-gardeners in regular work had a cottage for themselves and their family. They might also be given a fuel allowance.

For gardens of less than an acre with a paddock of three or four acres for a horse or cow, it was common to employ just one gardener, who did not live in but was paid on a weekly basis. He did all the necessary work in the garden, milking the cow, feeding the poultry and perhaps also looking after the horse. Samuel and Sarah Adams note that these people were generally 'under-gardeners from large establishments or from market gardens near large towns'.

The gardener for Anne Boulton's household at Thornhill was one of three men-servants employed there. According to Shena Mason in *The Hardware Man's Daughter*, from 1824 the gardener was Thomas Davenport and he rented a cottage somewhere in the grounds, where he lived with his wife. He was paid £3 14s per month and was entitled to a quart of beer a day, but no ale. Once a quarter, his cottage rent of £3 5s was deducted from his month's wages, but the couple were able to earn some extra income because Mrs Davenport occasionally did some work for Anne in the house.

The Gamekeeper

The gamekeeper was an integral part of the outdoor staff on a large country estate but the number kept depended on the size of the estate. A head keeper supervised the work of the gamekeepers beneath him and each keeper had his own 'beat'.

A H Bryer was the son of a head gamekeeper to Lord Leconfield, at a time when there were twenty-four keepers on the estate. In *The Day Before Yesterday*, he recalled: 'Although my father earned only fifteen shillings a week, and his cottage, we were never pushed for anything, in fact we were comfortably off. We always had enough clothes, and there was as much to eat as we wanted . . . in those days, there were rabbits and they were the keeper's to do what he liked with.' At the time, the rent for the cottage was around three shillings per week.

After leaving school at the age of 12, Bryer started work as a keeper boy earning seven shillings a week, and was trained by his father. He explained: '. . . it was a life you had to enjoy to take it up, for it was . . . seven days a week all the year round.' He stayed there for two years, and then moved 'to where I could earn fourteen shillings and a suit of clothes'.

He returned to keepering on the Leconfield estate after the First World War: 'I had two pounds ten a week, my cottage, a hundred faggots and a load of wood, and all the rabbits on my beat.' He was given an extra pound for training two black Labrador puppies every year.

The gamekeeper's duties included trapping all vermin, such as stoats, weasels, moles and rabbits, and shooting hawks, magpies and crows. Foxes could not be shot because the land was used for fox hunting. Rearing pheasants for the shooting season was another important responsibility of the gamekeeper. Weekend shooting parties were popular on large country estates in the Edwardian era, and there was usually a big shoot at Christmas too. The woodsmen on the estate acted as beaters.

Poaching was another issue the gamekeeper had to deal with, and each one had his own tried and tested methods. Bryer preferred not to get the police involved:

> When I was a young keeper, poachers were local men. With rabbit poaching I never interfered . . . but when it was a pheasant something had to be done . . . more often than not, I didn't hand the man over to the police, for times were hard, and often I knew the man was out of work through no fault of his own, and was poaching to earn something to keep his wife and family. So what I did was give the fellow a good hiding and take away his gun . . . My beatings and taking the guns often did better than a magistrate's sentence.

Chapter 11

FEMALE SERVANTS

The Housekeeper

At the top of the social hierarchy of female servants was the housekeeper. She was an upper servant who wore a chatelaine, to which was attached a large bunch of keys – a visible symbol of the trust placed in her by her employer. It was also a very audible sign to the other servants that she was on her way!

Writing in his memoir *What the Butler Winked At*, Eric Horne recalled that in the 1860s, 'The housekeeper . . . wore a black silk dress, a little silk apron trimmed with beads, a lace collar, and a large gold brooch, and a black velvet bow on top.' He added: 'The under-maids were more afraid of her than her Ladyship.'

A housekeeper could start in service as a housemaid or parlourmaid and work her way up, or could even be promoted from lady's maid, although this was less common because she needed experience of kitchen work. In her *Book of Household Management*, Mrs Beeton stressed that a housekeeper must bring to the management of a household 'all those qualities of honesty, industry and vigilance, in the same degree as if she were at the head of *her own* family.' She continued: 'Cleanliness, punctuality, order and method, are essentials in the character of a good housekeeper.'

It was the responsibility of the housekeeper to oversee the work of the servants, and that they were comfortable, but at the same time to check that their duties were being properly performed. As such, she had a difficult balance to strike. She had to maintain her authority by making sure she had no 'undue familiarity' with them, but at the same time, she needed to be approachable to the staff.

In addition, the housekeeper needed a thorough understanding of accounts because she had to record in her books all the sums paid, including the tradesmen's bills and other expenses of the house. Her role was mainly connected with the running of the house, and she dealt with cleaning,

Carte de visite of an unidentified servant, probably a housekeeper, circa 1880. Author's collection

heating and lighting, as well as the ordering and supply of materials, which often included food.

In a country house, a housekeeper's role included looking after the house while the family was away and preparing it for their return home at a few days' notice. She was in charge of all the female servants and was the head of the entire household if the steward or butler were away with the family. In households without a steward or man-cook, she prepared the confectionery, and attended to the preserving and pickling of fruits and vegetables. In smaller households, the role of cook and housekeeper was often combined.

In *Upstairs and Downstairs: Life in an English Country House*, Edward Hayward comments that housekeepers in stately homes could pocket fees from tourists when they showed them round. He cites the example of Mrs Hulme, housekeeper at Warwick Castle, who in the early nineteenth century, 'accumulated £30,000 in wages and gratuities.' Although there were a number of different ways in which a housekeeper could supplement her income, Mrs Hulme's extraordinary wealth was exceptional.

The Lady's Maid

A position as a lady's maid was a coveted one in a large country estate or a wealthy household in town. As a member of the 'upper servants', she held a high status within the household. Like the valet, the lady's maid was a personal servant to her mistress and took care of her wardrobe, hair and jewellery. As such, she needed a number of different attributes in order to satisfy her mistress's every whim.

Essential skills included dressmaking, hairdressing, millinery and packing. As a result of the dressmaking requirement, the route into working as a lady's maid was slightly different to the other servants. Experience as a seamstress or in a haberdasher's or milliner's could be sufficient to gain entry. Alternatively, a housemaid with dressmaking experience might 'better herself' by becoming a lady's maid, especially if she had proved herself as an asset in the household and could therefore offer impeccable references. This was, however, a far more difficult move.

A prospective lady's maid would usually start off working as a 'young lady's maid' (also sometimes known as 'schoolroom maid'): that is, a maid to the young daughter(s) of the mistress. She could then work her way up to 'lady's maid' although it would probably entail moving between jobs.

Born in Yorkshire in 1899, Rosina Harrison, who later became lady's maid to Lady Astor, had lessons in French and dressmaking even though 'it meant that I should earn no money until I got my first job, that instead of contributing to the family coffers I should be a drain on them.' When she left school at 16, she became an apprentice in a large dressmaking establishment. In her biography *Rose: My Life in Service*, she recalled that, two years later, her mother approached an agency to find out if there were any vacancies as 'young ladies' maids'. At the age of 18, she moved to London for her first job in service as a maid to the young daughters of the Tuftons, who lived in Mayfair.

The lady's maid was in charge of her mistress's wardrobe at all times, including the clothing which was taken on holiday, to London for the season, or when visiting other country houses. This important role meant she always travelled with her mistress. Careful packing of all the items was essential to ensure they reached their destination in the same condition in which they left.

Unlike other servants in the household, the lady's maid was allowed to take an interest in fashion and, in fact, one of the perquisites of the job was that she was given her mistress's cast-off clothing. In *The Victorian Domestic Servant*, Trevor May points out that when her mistress died, a lady's maid 'might expect to inherit the whole wardrobe, with the exception of items of lace, fur, velvet or satin.' Lady's maids were often resented by the other servants because of the airs and graces they assumed.

Some lady's maids were foreign, it being regarded that French or Swiss maids were of the highest calibre. French lady's maids were believed to have the most knowledge about fashion but they were thought to be more temperamental than their Swiss counterparts.

As a personal servant, the lady's maid had to attend to her mistress whenever she needed to change her clothes or dress her hair. In a household which entertained guests regularly, this could mean at least three changes of clothing per day. The lady's maid could not go to bed until her mistress retired for the night as she had to help her undress. When evening parties or balls occurred, she therefore had to work long hours and often did not finish until the early hours of the morning.

The lady's maid also had to wash the lace and fine linen of her mistress and keep all the items of clothing in good repair. Writing in the *Cornhill Magazine* (July 1901), Mrs Earle commented that 'in the early years of married life a lady's maid, besides being a great comfort, partly pays herself by the saving of dressmakers' bills, and turning old things into new. The lady's maid, too, must undertake the mending of house linen, an important duty, as very few housemaids can be trusted to do fine needlework at all.'

One heavy task was to bring up hot water for her mistress in the morning and at other times of the day, when required. *The Servants' Practical Guide* added that 'When ladies keep a pet dog or dogs, it is the duty of a lady's maid to attend to them; wash them, feed them and take them out walking.'

The lady's maid was often the only other person to have free access to her mistress's boudoir. As Edward Hayward comments, she 'had the task of ensuring that her mistress's appearance was always appropriate and immaculate; that, in time, grey hairs, wrinkles and a spreading figure were kept at bay and that minor ailments did not come in the way of a sparkling public persona.'

The older a lady's maid became, the harder it was to keep her position since a youthful appearance was preferred. According to Trevor May, 'a lack of knowledge of cookery and other aspects of domestic management' limited her chances of becoming a housekeeper and also of gaining offers of marriage. Edward Hayward, however, points out that 'she could well have saved enough to open a haberdasher's or milliner's shop in a fashionable part of the West End of London.'

The Cook

In domestic service, there were two kinds of female cook: 'professed' and 'plain'. A 'professed' cook could command a much higher salary as she was experienced enough to be able to produce complicated and fancy dishes. She did not have to do any cleaning or any plain cooking, for instance, for the servants, and all the ingredients were prepared for her by the kitchen-maid. Generally, she was employed in wealthy households or large country houses.

A 'plain' cook, on the other hand, had no kitchen-maid to help her. She was more likely to be employed in a small middle-class household with just one other servant on the staff, usually a housemaid or parlourmaid. Her salary was much lower than the 'professed' cook, and cleaning was part of her daily duties. In homes where only a cook and housemaid were employed, the cook was in charge of the dining-room, so she had to clean the hall, lamps and doorstep. All the cleaning had to be done before breakfast, which she then had to bring in for the family. She was also required to wait at the table and answer any bells in the morning, making the task of cooking even more difficult.

In her *Book of Household Management*, Mrs Beeton warned of the necessity for cooks and their assistants to be early risers 'for an hour lost in the morning, will keep her toiling, absolutely toiling, all day, to overtake that which might otherwise have been achieved with ease.' She suggested that in large establishments, the cook should rise at 6 am in the summer, and 7 am in winter. This was particularly necessary when a grand dinner had to be prepared.

In large households, the cook had breakfast in the housekeeper's room, but in some establishments she was also the housekeeper, in which case she made tea for the upper servants' breakfast. The cook supervised the breakfast for the family and directed the kitchen-maid to make the servants' breakfast.

After this, she drew up a menu on a slate for the day's luncheon and dinner, which *The Servants' Practical Guide* (1880) recommended should be 'according to the contents of the larder, and with due regard for variety'. The slate was either delivered to the mistress by the footman or the cook took it to her personally.

In *The Day Before Yesterday*, Margaret Thomas recalled working as a kitchen-maid in London in the 1900s before she became a cook. The slate 'was always written in French, so I spent most of my afternoons, until I got a working knowledge of the language, studying the cookery book, which gave the names of each dish in French as well as in English.'

The relationship between cooks and their mistresses was often a fragile one, and *The Servants' Practical Guide* (1880) commented that 'Some ladies stand very much in awe of their cooks, knowing that those who consider themselves to be thoroughly experienced will not brook fault-finding, or interference with their manner of cooking, and give notice on the smallest pretext.'

The cook was expected to keep the kitchen spotlessly clean or to supervise her assistants in cleaning it. In *The Complete Servant*, Samuel and Sarah Adams stressed that, 'Cleanliness, in every branch of domestic concerns cannot be too forcibly inculcated, and in the business of a Cook, particularly, it becomes a CARDINAL VIRTUE. Cleanliness and neatness of person and dress are not less important in her than the arrangement of the kitchen and larder, and all her operations.' Writing almost forty years later, Mrs Beeton agreed: 'Cleanliness is the most essential ingredient in the art of cooking; a dirty kitchen being a disgrace both to mistress and maid.'

The experienced cook not only understood the business of the kitchen, but she was also a good judge of provisions. This was particularly important in smaller households where there was no housekeeper, meaning she would have to go to market. She usually ordered goods from the tradesmen for the house and had to keep meticulous accounts of expenses, examining, checking and paying the tradesmen's bills once a month. She was usually paid commission by them when the books were paid.

At Himley Hall in Staffordshire, the housekeeper and cook role was combined. In 1820, Jane Sibson, the housekeeper at the time, was paid £47 14s 7d 'for Butter Sold' during the year. This amounted to more than her annual salary of £47 5s. (DE/IV/10/2 Ledgers 1817–1823, Dudley Archives and Local History Service)

The cook's morning duties included making the pastry, jellies, creams, and entrées for the dinner menu, and any similar dishes to be served at luncheon, soups for the following day, and dishing up the luncheon for the family. If there was no dinner party to prepare for and no other guests in the house, the cook had an easy afternoon.

Between the hours of five and nine in the evening were her busiest times because of the arduous nature of dishing up a dinner of many courses. If she had kitchen-maids to help her, the cook's work was over once the dinner was served as they did all the clearing and washing up.

A formal dinner was always five or six courses, but could be extended to as many as nine or ten. According to Trevor May in *The Victorian Domestic Servant*, a full-length dinner for eighteen people 'might well generate five hundred separate items of glassware, china, cutlery and kitchenware to be cleaned.'

In her *Book of Household Management*, Mrs Beeton commented: 'Everything must be timed so as to prevent its getting cold, whilst great care should be taken, that, between the first and second course, no more time is allowed than is necessary, for fear that the company in the dining-room lose all relish for what has yet to come of the dinner.'

For a dinner party, everything was prepared in the kitchen by the cook, but in some households, the butler was in charge of the salads and desserts in his pantry. The cook made all the etceteras for the table including pastry sticks, candies and salted almonds.

Margaret Powell got her first job as cook after working as a kitchen-maid in the 1920s. In her memoir *Below Stairs*, she recalled that not even her employer's parsimonious attitude could dampen her spirits:

The difference in status can only be understood by somebody who's been in domestic service. As a kitchen-maid you're a nobody, a nothing, you're not listened to, you're a skivvy for the other servants. All right, as a cook with only two other servants, you're not looked upon as God Almighty, but I didn't want that. I didn't want to be better than everybody else, I just wanted not to have somebody continually carping all the time at me.

In order to improve her skills, Margaret took cookery lessons at Leon's Grand School of Continental Cookery, paid for from her own pocket. She explained: 'The lessons were cheap, 2s 6d for a class lesson and 5s for a private one. I took the six class lessons first. Monsieur Leon . . . taught us to make some marvellous things out of very little.' This pleased her employer greatly, but the lessons ended abruptly when Margaret discovered that Monsieur Leon was not French at all!

Martha Agnes Rose Taylor, Cook

Born in Wolverhampton in 1854, Martha Agnes Rose Taylor was the

daughter of a shoemaker. By the time of the 1871 census, 16-year-old Martha was working as a housemaid for Reverend Charles Smith, the rector of Carlton, Nottinghamshire. It is likely she would have had one or two positions before this one, probably in her hometown. In this household, there was one other servant: Sarah Smith, an 18-year-old kitchen-maid from Essington, not far from Wolverhampton. There was also a woman acting as a sick nurse, presumably for the elderly rector or his wife.

It is possible that Martha found this position at the rectory through Sarah Smith, as they were both from the Wolverhampton area. Alternatively,

Photograph of Martha Agnes Rose Taylor, cook, circa 1880. Courtesy of Alan Mackie

it could have been advertised in a newspaper or she may have been recommended for the position by her own vicar.

From the documentary evidence, it appears that Martha did not take to the role of housemaid. The kitchen was the place she preferred and by the time of the next census in 1881, she was working as a cook for Caroline Augusta, Countess of Mount Edgcumbe at Cotehele Mansion in Calstock, Cornwall (now run by the National Trust). This would have been a huge step up for Martha. To achieve this position, she would have started as a lowly kitchen-maid and learned from the cooks she served under. After gaining sufficient knowledge and experience, she probably applied for a position as a cook in a small household before moving on to a larger establishment.

What makes this even more remarkable is that less than five months earlier, in November 1880, Martha had given birth to an illegitimate daughter, Dora, at the Queen Charlotte's Hospital, London, a charitable lying-in hospital for unmarried mothers. The hospital records reveal that Dora was delivered by forceps on 28 November, and that mother and baby left on 10 December.

On Dora's birth certificate, Martha's occupation was given as kitchen-maid, but it is possible that she had been working as a cook prior to her pregnancy and had to leave when her condition became evident. She could have found temporary work as a kitchen-maid up until the birth. No father is named on the birth certificate, but, tellingly, Martha gave Dora the middle name of Carlisle.

It would have been impossible for Martha to work in her profession of cook with a young child to look after, and it is unlikely Martha's new employer was aware of Dora's existence. At first, Dora became a 'nurse child' in the household of an unemployed tile-layer in London, where she was recorded on the 1881 census. The extra money for looking after Dora would have been very handy to this family, but she did not stay with them.

Dora was brought up by Martha's brother Herbert and his wife Emma in Wolverhampton as their own daughter. They had five children themselves and, unlike her cousins, Dora was educated until the age of 18 at a girls' school in Whitmore Reans. This expense was paid from a trust fund provided by her mysterious father in return for his anonymity. Dora always believed that Herbert and Emma were her parents and that Martha was her aunt. She did not find out the truth until Martha died in 1906.

Whatever the facts were, Martha must have earned a good salary as a cook to be able to provide for her daughter, especially in a wealthy place like Cotehele. The evidence suggests she arrived there not long after Dora was christened but before the census was taken on 3 April 1881, joining a staff of thirteen indoor servants, including a butler, two footmen, a coachman and a page. The variety of birthplaces of the indoor servants is striking. To obtain the best place with a good salary and living conditions, servants had to be prepared to move around the country.

It is not known how long Martha stayed at Cotehele or what prompted her to leave, but by 1891 she had moved back to London to work as a cook for Herbert Norman, a barrister in Southwell Gardens, Kensington. He kept a staff of seven servants including Martha, a butler and footman. With a good reference from the Countess of Mount Edgcumbe at Cotehele, Martha would have found it relatively easy to get a position in another wealthy household like this.

In 1894, Martha's life changed again when, at the age of 40, she married Frederick Sparkes, a butler who was eight years younger. It is believed they emigrated to America, possibly in 1896, but it appears the marriage was not a happy one and Martha returned to Britain alone.

She was in London, listed as Martha Sparkes, lodging house keeper, on the 1901 census; Frederick is nowhere to be seen. She must have kept in touch with members of staff at Cotehele she had known twenty years earlier, as one of her lodgers was 19-year-old Alfred Knight – he was the son of Richard Knight, the coachman at Cotehele.

By the time of her death in December 1906, Martha was again working as a cook, this time at a house in Forest Row, Sussex. It was there that she died of 'Syncope from fatty degeneration of the heart' and an inquest was held, presumably because the death was sudden. Martha was just 52 years old. Prior to her death, she sent three trunks of her belongings to a relative's house. Although she had wanted her estate to go to her daughter Dora, she did not leave a will. As she was still officially married to Frederick Sparkes, he was entitled to her estate. An advertisement was placed in a New York newspaper, where he was believed to be living, and he claimed the estate, valued at £141 8s 11d.

Dora was called to a solicitor's office in London, and it was at this point she found out she was the illegitimate daughter of Martha, and not her niece as she had always believed. She was allowed to choose one piece of Martha's jewellery and was given money to cover her and her husband's expenses in getting to and from London. Dora was also told about the trust fund which had been set up by her anonymous father after her birth, and was given a sum of money from the fund with the proviso that she never enquired who he was.

(With thanks to Alan Mackie for this information about his great-grandmother and grandmother.)

The Kitchen-Maid

The role of kitchen-maid was usually taken by those who wanted to progress to become a cook. This was because she was the cook's personal assistant and could learn a great deal simply by working for her. For this reason, she was sometimes known as an 'under-cook'.

A correspondent to the *Pall Mall Gazette* (24 May 1865) suggested that 'a head kitchen-maid with a good character from a good house, generally makes a far better cook for a moderate family than a professed cook and housekeeper, formidable on account of excessive experience.' This was usually because the professed cook was used to extravagant quantities and was not accustomed to economising.

This appears to be backed up by Miss Collet's *Report on the Money Wages of Indoor Domestic Servants*, (1899) which found that in two-servant and three-servant households, the cook 'has sometimes previously served an apprenticeship as kitchen-maid, but has more frequently specialised as a cook after experience as a general servant or "picked up" her knowledge when housemaid.'

The kitchen-maid was in charge of the majority of food preparation, including fish, poultry and vegetables, trimming meat joints and cutlets, and roasting, boiling and dressing all plain joints and dishes. She also cooked all the servants' meals and those for the schoolroom and nursery if there was one.

Writing in 1825, Samuel and Sarah Adams stressed that 'cleanliness must be considered as the *first and leading principle* of the kitchen-maid.' If a scullery maid was not employed, the kitchen-maid would also have to light the kitchen fires and keep the kitchen, larder, scullery and all the utensils clean, as well as the passages leading to the kitchen, the servants' hall and the front step of the house. She also had to scour the dressers, shelves and kitchen tables.

When Margaret Thomas was appointed as kitchen-maid in the 1900s in a house off London's Portman Square, she was paid £20 a year. She had to keep the butler's and footman's bedrooms clean, as they were in the basement, but she did not have to clean her own room because that was the under-housemaid's duty. In *The Day Before Yesterday*, she recalled: 'My duties consisted of waiting on the cook, preparing the food for her . . . cooking all the vegetables, roasts and savouries, making toast and coffee, and all pounding and chopping, all the staff cooking, and of course, sieving and washing up . . .'

Margaret Powell's first place was as kitchen-maid in Hove in the 1920s. In her memoir *Below Stairs*, she remembered the long list of duties she was given on her first day: 'I thought they had made a mistake. I thought it was for six people to do.' There was a 'hard old lump of blacklead' to do the grate with but no-one told her that it needed to be soaked overnight before 'it would assume any kind of a paste'.

In the kitchen was a huge dresser with 'a hundred and twenty-six pieces of china ranged on the shelves', plus 'an enormous soup tureen, vegetable dishes, and sauce boats. It was my job . . . to take this whole lot down once a week and wash every single piece of it, and scrub the dresser.'

One of the kitchen-maid's jobs was to lay out the cook's table twice a day. Margaret Powell commented: 'There were knives of all kinds . . . big long carving knives, small knives for paring fruit, pallet knives, bent knives for scraping out basins with, and then metal spoons . . . the largest ones had the measures on them, from ounces right up to dessert-spoonfuls.'

Also laid out on the table were a hair sieve and a wire sieve, a flour sifter, an egg whisk, two kinds of graters (a fine one for nutmegs and the other for breadcrumbs), large and small chopping boards, three or four basins, paprika pepper, cayenne pepper, ordinary salt, pepper and vinegar. Many of the items were used two or three times when preparing a meal, so the kitchen-maid had to wash them quickly ready for the cook.

The Scullery Maid

While the kitchen-maid's role was to assist the cook in the preparation of food, the scullery maid's main tasks involved cleaning. In larger households, she was employed to keep the scullery, larders, kitchen passages, servants' hall, housekeeper's room and steward's room spotlessly clean and tidy, plus the front step of the house. The scullery was where all the washing up was done, except for the best china and glass, which were cleaned in the housekeeper's room and butler's pantry respectively.

It was the scullery maid's responsibility to wash up all the dishes and to clean all the saucepans, stew-pans, kettles, pots and other kitchen utensils, which were usually washed in soda and water, then scoured. These had to be ready for use straight away if the cook needed them. Copper pans and moulds were often scoured with a mixture of sand, salt, vinegar and flour rubbed on by hand.

One of her most important and arduous tasks was to black the kitchen range and light it first thing in the morning, as well as to light the fires under the copper or boilers. The scullery maid ate in the kitchen with the kitchen-maids, instead of in the servants' hall. According to Samuel and Sarah Adams, the scullery maid might also be expected to make the beds for the stable men and to fetch, carry and clear away for the cook and kitchen-maid, 'and otherwise assist in all the laborious parts of the kitchen business.'

A post as a scullery maid was the bottom rung of the ladder in the kitchen, but as Mrs Beeton pointed out in her *Book of Household Management*, 'if she be fortunate enough to have over her a good kitchen-maid and clever cook, she may very soon learn to perform various little duties connected with cooking operations, which may be of considerable service in fitting her for a more responsible place.'

The Parlourmaid

Laying the table, waiting at meals, answering the door and announcing visitors were probably the most important of a parlourmaid's duties. As such, she was undertaking many of the tasks a footman would carry out in a larger household.

According to *The Servants' Practical Guide* (1880), large numbers of people preferred to employ a parlourmaid instead of a male servant: 'Ladies who do not have the support of a male relative in everyday life find it less trouble to keep their household in order when it is composed of female servants only, as a man-servant is proverbially inclined to take advantage of his position when there is no master to keep him in check.' It was also more economical because a parlourmaid's wages were lower than a man-servant's: she was not subject to tax and there were no associated livery costs. During the morning, the parlourmaid wore a cotton gown with a white apron and cap, and in the afternoon (when answering the door and receiving visitors) she changed into a stuff gown with apron and cap.

If no lady's maid was employed, the parlourmaid was also expected to take on the role of looking after her mistress's wardrobe and helping her to dress. In addition, according to the *Servants' Practical Guide* (1880), she had to help with 'getting-up the fine linen of the ladies of the family'. In the afternoon, she carried out various needlework tasks.

The Housemaid

The housemaid had a long list of seemingly never-ending duties, the most difficult of which included cleaning the grates and lighting the fires in the drawing-room, dining-room, other sitting-rooms and bedrooms. She was also required to sweep, dust and polish in these rooms, as well as the

Carte de visite of an unidentified servant, probably a housemaid, circa 1885. Author's collection

servants' bedrooms, the front staircase and front hall; she had to make all the beds and empty the chamber-pots (including those of the servants). If no lady's maid or valet was employed, the housemaid had to carry up water for each of the family to have a bath.

During the afternoon, there was plenty of tidying to be done and also a little sewing. Throughout the day, she had to make sure that every bedroom was supplied with sufficient candles, soap, clean towels and writing paper. If fires were kept going in the bedrooms during the day, she had to attend to them. In the evening, it was the housemaid's duty to prepare the bedrooms for the night by turning down the beds, closing the curtains and filling the jugs with water. Her final task of the day was to take a can of hot water up to each bedroom and dressing room.

In many large households, housemaids were not meant to be seen by the family. In *The Victorian Domestic Servant*, Trevor May comments that at Crewe Hall in Cheshire, it was 'stipulated that no housemaid was ever to be seen, other than in chapel' and that the tenth Duke of Bedford 'was liable to dismiss any maid who unwittingly crossed his path after midday, by which time all housework was supposed to have been completed.'

In a large country house, there might be two, three or even four housemaids and there was a strict hierarchy of duties between them. When there was a fourth housemaid, she usually dealt exclusively with the servants' rooms. The head housemaid did light jobs only, but they all did sewing in the afternoon.

When comparing the working hours of housemaids, factory girls and shopwomen, Jessie Boucherett, writing in *Englishwoman's Review* (1873), concluded that the housemaid worked the hardest. She broke down the working hours like this:

A housemaid is usually required to begin work soon after six o'clock am and goes to bed after ten pm. She has for rest, half an hour for breakfast, an hour for dinner, and half an hour each for tea and supper, in all two hours and a half for meals, and in the afternoon she is generally required to do needlework for an hour and a half, which may fairly be regarded as rest, giving altogether four hours' rest. This leaves twelve hours of actual work, longer by two hours than the day's work of factory women, and longer than the usual day's work of a shopwoman.

In addition, the housemaid's work was of a more severe nature, because she had to carry coals and water, and to lift heavy weights in making beds and emptying baths. She only had partial rest on Sunday, compared with the factory girl's and shopwoman's complete day off. Mondays were particularly difficult for her in families where the washing was done at home as she was 'often required to rise at three or four in the morning to help the laundry-maid'.

To put this into perspective, Jessie Boucherett commented that 'it is well known that a housemaid's work is considered lighter than that of a cook, kitchen-maid, scullery maid, or dairymaid . . .'

In her *Book of Household Management*, Mrs Beeton emphasised that the amount of additional work servants, especially housemaids, could cope with, depended on the season:

> As, in the winter months, servants have much more to do, in consequence of the necessity there is to attend to the number of fires throughout the household, not much more than the ordinary everyday work can be attempted. In the summer, and when the absence of fires gives the domestics more leisure, then any extra work that is required can be more easily performed.

The Stillroom Maid

The stillroom was a specialist area of a large country house, and would not normally have been found in a smaller establishment. It was traditionally overseen by the housekeeper. According to Edward Hayward in *Upstairs and Downstairs: Life in an English Country House*, the name of the room derives from 'a distilling apparatus for making special concoctions from fruits, herbs, spices and sugar, which were used for cleaning, flavouring, colouring, and curing small ailments'.

The stillroom maid was the housekeeper's personal servant, and her general duties included lighting the fire, dusting the room, preparing the breakfast-table and waiting at the different meals taken in the housekeeper's room. She also assisted her in all manner of other tasks, including distilling aromatic waters, spirits and oils; making essences and perfumes; making pickles, preserves, pastry and confectionery; making coffee for upstairs; preparing light sweets and ices, fruit wines and cordials; making simple medicines from herbs and spices; washing the china; and managing and arranging the store-room.

In her *Book of Household Management*, Mrs Beeton commented that 'a stillroom maid may learn a very great deal of useful knowledge from her intimate connection with the housekeeper, and if she be active and intelligent, may soon fit herself for a better position in the household.'

The Maid of All Work/General Servant

A maid of all work or general servant was one of the most common types of servant found in small middle-class households. According to Mrs Beeton, she was 'perhaps the only one of her class deserving of commiseration: her life is a solitary one, and, in some places, her work is never done'. She added: 'She is also subject to rougher treatment than either the house or kitchen-maid, especially in her earlier career: she starts in life, probably a girl of thirteen, with some small tradesmen's wife as her mistress, just a step above her in the social scale . . .'

The fact that employer and servant was so close to one another in terms of social class meant that everything possible was done to define the line between them. To this end, a maid of all work was usually expected to eat and sleep by herself. While this was considered necessary to maintain the order and structure of the household, it must have made these servants feel very lonely and isolated.

On top of this, a great deal of work was expected from her as she had to perform all the duties a cook, kitchen-maid and housemaid would carry out in larger establishments. Her tasks might also include the arduous task of washing once a week. However, Mrs Beeton was adamant that 'if the washing, or even a portion of it, is done at home, it will be impossible for the maid of all work to do her household duties thoroughly, during the time it is about, unless she have some assistance.'

If the washing was done at home and not sent out to a laundry, she urged the mistress to hire someone to assist at the wash-tub, and to see to 'little matters herself, in the way of dusting, clearing away breakfast things, folding, starching, and ironing the fine things. With a little management much can be accomplished, provided the mistress be industrious, energetic, and willing to lend a helping hand.'

By 1899, when Miss Collet wrote her *Report on the Money Wages of Indoor Domestic Servants*, she discovered that

> . . . it is the almost universal practice either to engage a laundress to do, or help to do, the washing at home or to send out the whole, or if not the whole the heaviest part of it, to a laundry. The general servant is hardly ever expected to do by herself any but very light washing for the reason given by one mistress: 'Washing is put out, as it is now almost impossible to get a girl who will do it.'

Miss Collet found that it was almost impossible for general servants in one-servant households to 'better themselves' and gain promotion to households employing many servants and paying higher wages. This was because of the lack of 'professional' training which she considered 'a serious defect in our social organisation'.

However, according to Miss Collet, '. . . the thoroughly good general servant can secure for herself such warm appreciation from the family she serves, that her privileges and freedom quite outweigh the attractions of better paid service in richer households.' For general servants at the bottom of the tree, such as the young 'slavey' of the lodging house or coffee shop, life was far more difficult and they had to 'work harder and under more unfavourable conditions perhaps than any other class of the community'.

The Dairymaid

According to Mrs Beeton, the duties of a dairymaid depended upon where she lived, as in 'Scotland, Wales and some of the northern counties, women milk the cows.' In private families in England, the cows were usually milked by a cow-keeper, while on large dairy farms, the dairymaid might be expected to assist with the milking.

Whether or not she milked the cows, the dairymaid's main role was to provide the house with milk, cream and butter 'and other luxuries'. Butter was usually churned twice or three times a week. Mrs Beeton advised the dairymaid that it would be 'advantageous in being at work on churning mornings by five o'clock'. Churning took anything from twenty minutes to half an hour in summer, but much longer in winter.

A steady uniform motion was required to produce sweet butter. Washing the butter with pure spring water, and repeatedly kneading and pouring off the water was the next stage, until it was perfectly free from milk. Mrs Beeton stressed: 'Imperfect washing is the frequent cause of bad butter, and in nothing is the skill of the dairymaid tested more than in this process; moreover, it is one in which cleanliness of habits and person are most necessary.'

After the churning and butter-making was finished, and the butter-milk had been disposed of, the dairymaid had to scald with boiling water every single utensil she had used. She was also required to brush out the churn, clean out the cream-jars, and wipe everything dry.

The Laundry-Maid

Laundry-maids were employed in large country houses to take care of all the household's washing. The laundry was separate from the house and usually consisted of a washing-house, an ironing room and a drying room. It was built near to the drying-ground and created a great deal of steam and unpleasant smells. From the 1850s, machinery to dry the clothing was gradually introduced. Traditionally, laundry-maids had rosy complexions because of the heat they were subjected to.

According to Trevor May in *The Victorian Domestic Servant*, 'Laundry-maids tended to be an independent group, not always under the control of the housekeeper . . . Their proximity to the groom-filled stables was recognised as a problem by some employers.'

As early as 1861, Mrs Beeton referred to the growing practice in large towns of sending laundry out to professional laundresses and laundry companies which used 'mechanical and chemical processes'. This was because there was 'little convenience for bleaching and drying'. As these processes were said to 'injure the fabric of the linen', many families chose to wash the fine linen, cottons and muslins at home, even when the bulk of the washing was sent out. In country houses and those in the suburbs, washing at home remained the norm for some time.

In her *Report on the Money Wages of Indoor Domestic Servants* (1899), Miss Collet found that employing laundry-maids or including laundry work as part of the duties in households where only two or three servants was kept was more common in Scotland than in England or Wales. In the latter, it had become 'the rule, except in large households with laundries of their own, and in households managed on narrow means, to send this work out'.

The Head Nurse

Known affectionately as 'Nanny' by the children under her care, the head nurse was one member of staff who was often retained by the family for the next generation. As one of the upper servants, the head nurse took her supper in the housekeeper's or steward's room.

According to Samuel and Sarah Adams in *The Complete Servant*, the head nurse 'ought to be of a lively and cheerful disposition, perfectly good tempered, and clean and neat in her habits and person.' For Mrs Beeton, 'patience and good temper' were 'indispensable qualities' required for this servant. She added: 'She ought also to be acquainted with the art of ironing and trimming little caps, and be handy with her needle.'

The head nurse had responsibility for the care and management of the young children in the family, and had sole charge of each infant from its birth as soon as it was weaned from its mother, or a wet nurse. The nursery wing

Postcard of an unidentified head nurse with the baby in her care, circa 1900. Author's collection

was under her entire control, and she directed the under-nurses to assist her with the work.

In the nursery wing, there was usually a day nursery and a night nursery, together with a small kitchen or pantry, plus a room for the under-nurse and nursery-maid to share. The head nurse slept in the night nursery next to the infant in her care.

She got up at about seven o'clock, ready to bathe the children. Until the age of about 5 their place was in the nursery, but after this time they went to the schoolroom in the mornings for lessons with a tutor or governess (who was not classed as a domestic servant). It was the head nurse's responsibility to supervise the sterilising of milk, the boiling of water and sieving of vegetables and fruit.

It was possible to become a head nurse by working up from the bottom as a nursery-maid, then as under-nurse before progressing to head nurse. An ambitious under-nurse would have to be prepared to move between posts in order to gain promotion, as head nurses were often 'old retainers' who had worked for their employers for a long period of time.

In *The Day Before Yesterday*, Sarah Sedgwick recalled that her first place in domestic service was as a nursery-maid at a large house near Doncaster in the Edwardian period, for which she was paid £10 a year. For her second position, she went to a house in Scarborough as an under-nurse for three children at £22 a year, and by the time she left, she had been promoted to head nurse at £30 a year.

The Under-Nurse

The under-nurse was expected to attend to the senior children, and was directed by the head nurse. She helped them to get up in the morning, washed and dressed them, gave them their meals, took them out for air and exercise, and assisted in all the duties of the nursery while the head nurse attended to the infant child. These other tasks might include bringing up and removing the nursery meals, making beds and mending clothing.

As part of the nursery staff, the under-nurse took her meals in the nursery with the nursery-maid, never mixing with the other servants or eating in the servants' hall. This underlined the separateness of the nursery from the rest of the house; for instance, it usually had its own china, silver and linen. If there was no other staff employed in the nursery, the under-nurse would also have to light the fires, empty the slops and sweep, scour and dust the rooms.

The Nursery-Maid

The nursery-maid was the youngest member of the nursery staff, and she had to rise between half past five and six o'clock. Her first duty was to light the fire and carry out household work in the nursery before the children got up.

As a nursery-maid in the 1900s, Sarah Sedgwick had to get up at 5.30 am to light the nursery fires and clean the fire guard before 7.30 am when she woke the head nurse with a cup of tea. In *The Day Before Yesterday*, she recalled 'how important time was in the nursery. Everything had to happen to the minute.'

Breakfast for the children was at 8.00 am, and between 10.00 and 12.30, they were taken out in the prams. Luncheon was at 1.00 pm, followed by another walk out between 2.00 and 3.30 pm. Tea was at 4.00 pm, after which the children were dressed to go downstairs and 'they were taken into the drawing-room to the minute, and brought up again to the minute.' There were then baths to be drawn for the children (with all the water brought upstairs) followed by bed. This regimental routine was mirrored downstairs where meal times were fixed for the rest of the family and the servants.

In addition to herself, there was a head nurse, under-nurse and a maid to wait on the nursery, 'and in the winter a footman who came up every two hours to make up the fires.' There were just two children in this nursery: a baby and a 2-year-old girl.

The huge number of layers worn by the children, and the numerous changes of clothing in a day created a great deal of work for the nursery staff. For instance, in the Edwardian period in winter, girls wore a vest, a woollen binder, drawers, a bodice, a flannel petticoat, and a cotton petticoat; and on top, flannel dresses.

A baby wore long clothes from birth until it was six weeks or two months old, then its clothes were shortened to foot length. Underneath there was a vest, woolly binder, mackintosh knickers over its nappy, woolly knickers, a long flannel which tied at the side with sarsnet ribbon, and an enormous starched petticoat. On top of that was a robe, a woolly coat and a bonnet. When taken outside the house, the baby wore a pelisse (a loose-fitting coat with a large cape collar).

Clothes were changed in the morning, in the afternoon and to go downstairs to the drawing-room to meet the children's parents. In addition, in wealthy households, children might start riding ponies from the age of 5, creating even more washing for the nursery staff, with specially made riding habits and boots.

As Sarah Sedgwick recalled,

It was the way children had to be turned out that made so much work. Although there was a laundress for large things, we did all the small washing, and the nappies, and of course all the children's mending. The clothes to be worn the next morning were always pressed overnight [and] ribbons had to be pressed before they were threaded . . . I was supposed to be in bed myself at 9.30, but that was something which could not always happen to the minute, for with the washing, ironing, and running in of ribbons, I couldn't get it done in time.

Part 4

SOURCES

Chapter 12

GENERAL SOURCES

The Census

The census is an official count of the population, and the first one in Britain was taken on 10 March 1801; a census has been taken every ten years since, except 1941. Censuses are usually closed for 100 years, and the dates on which the currently available census returns were taken are 6 June 1841; 30 March 1851; 7 April 1861; 2 April 1871; 3 April 1881; 5 April 1891; 31 March 1901; and 2 April 1911.

The first useful census for family historians is the one taken in 1841, as the previous returns were mainly for statistical purposes. However, this census does not provide as much information as those in later years because the ages of adults over 15 were rounded down to the nearest five years, and places of birth were not given – simply an 'N' for no and 'Y' for yes in answer to the question 'Were you born in this county?' In addition, if someone was a servant, the enumerator often just wrote 'M.S.' (male servant) or 'F.S.' (female servant), without giving the precise occupation; in some cases, in the section for name, none is given.

Later census returns give the full address, the full name of the householder and everyone in the household (plus their relationship to the head of the house); their ages, condition as to marriage, place of birth and occupation; if blind, deaf or dumb (and later, if an idiot or lunatic). From 1891, information is given about the number of rooms occupied if less than five, and whether individuals were an employer, employed or neither. This was slightly changed in 1901 to read 'Employer, Worker or Own Account' or 'Working at Home'. The 1911 census provides even more information about rooms in the house. It asked for 'the Number of Rooms in this Dwelling (House, Tenement or Apartment). Count the kitchen as a room but do not count scullery, landing, lobby, closet, bathroom; nor warehouse, office, shop.'

On the census, each place was divided into a number of enumeration districts covered by individual enumerators, so unless you use an online search facility, you will need to know roughly where your ancestor was living.

Census returns for England and Wales are freely available at The National Archives, and for specific areas at county record offices and large city libraries. Scottish census returns can be accessed at the ScotlandsPeople Centre (www.scotlandspeoplehub.gov.uk/index) or at county record offices.

You can also see census returns on many commercial family history websites on a subscription or pay-per-view basis. Many archives and libraries subscribe to these websites, so it is often possible to use the service for free. The beauty of this format is that it makes the census easily searchable by place or name, but be aware it is always possible that your ancestor's name was incorrectly transcribed, leading to a 'not found' scenario.

The census is extremely useful because it may be the only source which identifies your ancestor's specific occupation, for example, second housemaid, under-butler, etc. It also shows the size of the household and the number of other staff, which provides two extra pieces of information: the likely income of the employer and the amount of work your ancestor was expected to do. If the number of rooms is given, this can also give an indication of the level of work required to maintain them.

If male senior staff had married and had families but were still required to live in at their employer's house, their wives and children will be found in a separate household on the census.

Bear in mind that if your female ancestor was of school age on one census and married by the next, there will be no record of her work as a domestic servant. However, if she was a working-class girl and was not living in an industrial area where mills or factories offered alternative employment, it is highly likely she did work in domestic service before marrying.

If your ancestor was a servant in a large country house, remember that the family (and some of the staff) decamped to their residence in the capital for the London season, or to a rented house. The season traditionally started after Easter and ended on 12 August (the 'Glorious Twelfth', when the grouse shooting season began). A skeleton staff was usually left at home to maintain and clean the country property. This frequently coincided with census time, so don't be surprised if your ancestor is not where you expect him or her to be.

The census also sometimes coincided with holiday time when some of the household might be staying at a seaside hotel or other resort. On the census, the servants who went with their employers are usually recorded separately from them, and from the resident staff. They are denoted as 'visitors' servants' but the census does not usually identify which servants belonged to which visitors.

For servants with families, look carefully at the birthplaces of their children. These may reveal different parts of the country in which your ancestor worked; relocating was often necessary to secure a better post with higher wages or more security.

The following is an example from the 1871 census showing the household at Erddig Hall, Denbighshire.

Name & Surname of each person	Relation to Head of family	Condition	Age		Rank, Profession or Occupation	Where Born
			Male	Female		
Simon Yorke	Head	Married	59		J P & Landowner	Erddig, Denbighshire
Victoria M L Yorke	Wife	Married		47		London
E Mary Anne Yorke	Daughter	Unmarried		23		Denbighshire
Philip Yorke	Son	Unmarried	21		Lieut. R D Militia	Denbighshire
A Susan Yorke	Daughter	Unmarried		16		Denbighshire
A Chevalier	Governess	Unmarried		30	Governess	Switzerland
George Dickinson	Butler	Married	37		Butler	Whitegate
Mary Webster	Servant	Widow		64	Housekeeper	Knockin
Harriett Rogers	Servant	Unmarried		38	Lady's Maid	[illegible]
Emilly Crane	Servant	Unmarried		24	Lady's Maid	Manchester
Ann Haines	Servant	Unmarried		56	House Maid	Upton on Severn
Ruth Davies	Servant	Widow		26	Dairy Maid	Marchwiel
Hannah Richards	Servant	Unmarried		20	Kitchen Maid	Stansty
M McGeary	Servant	Unmarried		23	Laundry Maid	Wrexham
Sarah Roberts	Servant	Unmarried		20	Housemaid	Ruabon
Joseph Sochattie	Servant	Unmarried	20		Footman	Braemar
Harry Hughes	Servant	Unmarried	17		Footman	Bangor, Denbighshire

Wills and Probate Records

A surprisingly large number of servants left wills or had household effects of a significant value when probate was granted. This applied particularly to senior staff such as cooks, housekeepers, butlers and valets. As board and lodging was provided for them, servants could, if they wished, save a considerable amount of money during their working lives, particularly if they were unmarried or widowed.

Born in 1840, Hannah Edwards became the housekeeper at Himley Hall,

Staffordshire at some point between 1871 and 1881. She was widowed between the 1861 and 1871 censuses, and on the latter she was recorded as a 'domestic servant cook'.

At the time, she had two young sons to look after so a live-in position as a housekeeper would not have been possible. Ten years later, however, her 17-year-old son William was working as a tailor in Birmingham while her younger son Robert was also employed at Himley Hall as the steward's room boy, aged 14.

Hannah Edwards remained as housekeeper at Himley until her death in October 1916, although by 1891 the role had become more like a caretaker as the Dudley family were spending more time elsewhere. On 28 December 1889, Hannah wrote a will and lodged it with a local solicitor. This is an extract:

I direct my Executor hereinafter named to pay all my just debts funeral and testamentary expenses as soon as convenient after my decease. I give all wearing apparel, jewellery, pictures and household ornaments to my three daughters namely Eliza the wife of Henry Roberts, Annie and Mary Elizabeth equally between them. I give & devise and bequeath all the rest residue and remainder of my personal estate and my real estate (if any) unto my five children the said Eliza Roberts, Annie, Mary Elizabeth, William George and Robert Kelsall share and share alike as tenants in common. And I declare that if the sum of Eighty pounds which I have advanced to my son William George together with any interest due thereon at the rate of two pounds ten shillings per centum per annum shall be due and owing at the time of my decease, the same is to be deducted from his share as aforesaid, and in case his said share is not of sufficient amount to pay the said loan of Eighty pounds and interest thereon then the balance shall be a debt due from my son William George and the same shall be recoverable by my said Executor accordingly. I appoint my son Robert Kelsall Edwards now residing at Pansanger in the County of Hertford Footman Sole Executor of this my Will . . .

(D/HF2/44 Will of Hannah Edwards, housekeeper, Himley Hall,
28 December 1889, Dudley Archives and Local History Service)

Although this is not a very detailed will in terms of listing out possessions, it tells us a lot about the family relationships in the Edwards family. It is clear that Hannah had amassed some savings in her time as housekeeper as she was able to lend her son William George £80. However, it is also evident that she wanted him to repay this loan plus interest so that his siblings would not lose out on their inheritance.

In fact, Hannah was predeceased by both her sons and one of her daughters. William George died in 1890 leaving personal effects worth £94 18s; it is not known if the loan was repaid by his widow. From steward's room boy in 1881, Robert Kelsall had progressed to become a house steward himself by the time of his marriage in 1899. Shortly afterwards, he set up as a licensed victualler but he died in 1913, three years before his mother. According to the National Probate Calendar, Hannah Edwards had effects valued at £1,151 2s 10d at the time of her death.

When a servant had worked for a family loyally and faithfully for a good number of years, he or she was often mentioned in the will when the master or mistress died. At the very least, bequests might include money for mourning clothes for servants to wear at the funeral. According to Pamela Sambrook in *Keeping Their Place*, 'one year's extra wages seems to have been usual for general servants, with special provision made for long-serving personal attendants.'

The most loyal and appreciated servants could receive bequests of treasured objects, stocks or shares, lump sums of money, annuities and even property. In many cases, this allowed the servant to retire, buying them their own independence. Do not assume, however, that if there is no mention of a formal bequest, the servant was forgotten. An informal arrangement was often made by the succeeding master or mistress, particularly if he or she wanted a 'changing of the guard' to install his own staff. The death of an employer could often lead to a period of uncertainty for the servants, particularly if relationships with the new master were strained.

Wills for England and Wales

If your ancestor left a will, it can be extremely useful in helping to determine family relationships. Before 12 January 1858, there was no national court for proving English and Welsh wills. Instead, they were proved in one of the church courts, of which there were more than 250. Most of these documents are held in county record offices – you can search Access to Archives (A2A) to find out about specific probate records held at individual archives (www.a2a.org.uk).

The National Archives holds the original indexes to wills and administrations of the Prerogative Court of Canterbury, catalogued under 'PROB 12'. You can also search them on Documents Online (www.national archives.gov.uk/documentsonline/wills.asp); a fee is payable to download each document.

Online will indexes for other church courts/record offices are listed on Your Archives (http://yourarchives.nationalarchives.gov.uk/index.php?title= Online_Probate_Indexes).

Wills proved in England and Wales from 12 January 1858 onwards are held by the Probate Service. The National Probate Calendar is an index of these wills and administrations; the full index can be seen at the London Probate Registry while partial indexes are available at The National Archives, the Guildhall Library, the Society of Genealogists and local probate registries. A list of these can be found on the Probate Registry website (www.hmcourts-service.gov.uk/infoabout/civil/probate/registries).

The entries in the National Probate Calendar give the full name, address and occupation of the deceased; the full names of executors, administrators and relationships to the deceased; the date and place of death, and of the granting of probate or administration; plus the value of the estate. An application for administration could be made if a person died without leaving a will and there were problems with the estate. If your ancestor left a will, it should have been proved within a year or two of his or her death. The National Probate Calendar has been digitised and is available through Ancestry (www.ancestry.co.uk).

Once you have the exact details of your ancestor's will or administration, you can apply for a copy in person at the London Probate Registry, or by post from the Leeds District Probate Registry (see the Useful Contacts section).

Wills for Scotland

In Scotland, the terminology for wills is slightly different. The term 'testament' is used to describe documents which relate to the executry (moveable property) of the deceased, including an inventory and, in a minority of cases, a will.

Testaments for the period 1514–1901 have been digitised, and can be seen at The National Archives of Scotland. Alternatively, you can search the free online index on the ScotlandsPeople website (www.scotlandspeople.gov.uk); a charge is made for buying copies of documents.

From 1902, there is an annual index of Scottish testaments called the Calendar of Confirmations. The calendar is available at The National Archives for Scotland in Edinburgh, and the Mitchell Library in Glasgow, which holds the index up to 1936.

Newspapers

Newspapers are invaluable for offering a window into the times in which your ancestor lived. More than this, they can provide additional information about your servant ancestor's working life in a number of different ways. The 'Situations Vacant' and 'Situations Wanted' columns are a goldmine in this respect. They would often have been the first port of call when a servant was looking for a new place. It was less common for servants to advertise their services since it cost them money to do so, but it did happen.

This very exacting advertisement from the *Daily News* (25 April 1900) is fascinating because it is so detailed:

WANTED, from Devonshire, an industrious, trustworthy, active, working HOUSEKEEPER, who thoroughly understands dairy, baking, curing hams and bacon, a good plain cook, and buttermaker. A General Servant, 25 years of age, kept. Three in family. One gentleman always in residence. Other gentlemen and lady about six months of the year, when four more servants come with them. Three cows kept. She must be able and willing to work, as the house must always be in the most perfect order, and have good references for being honest, an abstainer, trustworthy and understanding her duties. Not under 35 years of age or over 45, and must like a quiet place in the country, five miles from town (near Essex) and station, and must enjoy strong health. Wages £20 a year, and all found. Address to Lady M., Box 196A. "Daily News" Inquiry Office, 57, Fleet-street, E.C. No letters will be answered that do not contain full name and address, where lived, how long, in what capacity, excuse of leaving, and enclosing photo, taken within the last twelve months, which will be returned.

Obituaries of long-serving members of staff may also be found in newspapers, especially in the early twentieth century. William John Morey was a butler and later a house steward for the Verney family at Claydon House, Buckinghamshire. His master was Harry Verney, baronet and landowner who was married to Parthenope, the sister of Florence Nightingale. As a result of this family relationship, William Morey knew Florence Nightingale, and was held in high regard by her.

LADY'S MAID LEARNING HAIR-DRESSING.

'Lady's Maid Learning Hairdressing: Servant London', Living London, 1902

The *Buckinghamshire Advertiser* printed an obituary for William when he died in April 1907:

DEATH OF MR W J MOREY

Mr William John Morey passed away at his residence in East Claydon early on Friday morning April 26th. He had for 33 years been in the service of the Verney family at Claydon House and only relinquished the duties of house steward about two months back through a severe attack of paralysis from which there appeared to be no chance of recovery and he gradually sank. Practically all our readers were familiar with the deceased, whose geniality and affability at all the many gatherings at Claydon House for years past was most highly appreciated.

Whether as Hon. Secretary on various committees or in other positions, his able help was always most readily given and it is certainly not too much to say that mainly through his efforts and instrumentality, success has been achieved by the almost innumerable gatherings that have taken place in the lovely gardens and grounds of Claydon House.

He was 57 years old and leaves a widow and son and daughter to mourn their deep loss . . .

A later issue reported on William Morey's funeral in great detail, even listing the messages accompanying the numerous wreaths. A key part of this report says: 'The coffin was of polished oak with brass breastplate on which was inscribed: William John Morey born 2 September 1849, died 26 April 1907.' This last piece of information illustrates how valuable newspaper reports can be as a birth certificate has not been found for William Morey. (With thanks to Carolyn Middleton for this information about her ancestor.)

When a will of a prominent landowner was made public, newspapers printed the information in their columns. These wills often included bequests for servants. In addition, newspapers published reports of incidents and criminal cases regarding servants in minute detail. Articles and letters about domestic servants, and how they were viewed by society, can also be read.

The trade press such as *The Gardeners' Chronicle, The Field, The Shooting Times, The Gamekeeper,* or *The Lady* are also useful sources of information on servants. The British Library holds all such publications; see the Useful Contacts section.

Many British Library national and local newspapers can be viewed and searched online at www.britishnewspaperarchive.co.uk or http://news papers.bl.uk/blcs – you may be lucky enough to find that the place you're interested in has been covered. If you local library subscribes to the latter resources, it may be possible to view it for free using your library card to log in. *The Times Digital Archive 1785–1985* is a similar resource which your library may subscribe to.

Alternatively, the local record office should hold copies of relevant newspapers and may even have name indexes to help narrow down the search. You can find out where your nearest archive is through ARCHON (www.nationalarchives.gov.uk/archon).

Trade Directories

Like today's telephone directories, old trade directories are made up of people offering goods and services in a particular area, who paid to be listed. They also include lists of private residents in a separate section from the trades. The directories were published for each county or large city, although late eighteenth- and early nineteenth-century directories often covered several counties in one volume.

If you want to find out whether there was a servants' registry office in the area in which your ancestor was working, look under 'Registry Offices' or 'Servants'. Trade directories can also be useful in tracing your ancestor after he or she retired from service, perhaps if they went into business running a pub or hotel, a milliner's or even a servants' registry office. Many retired male upper servants ended their lives listed in their local trade directory as 'gentlemen', simply because they were annuitants living on their own means.

A useful online source of old trade directories is the Historical Directories project at www.historicaldirectories.org. A selection from a number of different counties and decades has been digitised, and you may find the area you are interested in has been covered. Most county record offices, archives or large city libraries hold copies of old trade directories. Some of the larger libraries even have collections which cover the whole country.

Criminal Records

If your servant ancestor had a brush with the law and was convicted of a criminal offence, you can try searching the prison records for him or her. Criminal registers for England and Wales 1791–1892 have been digitised on Ancestry (www.ancestry.co.uk), and the Old Bailey trial records are also available online (www.oldbaileyonline.org).

Poor Law Records

If a child was an inmate in a workhouse (or poorhouse in Scotland), or in an industrial school administered by the workhouse, he or she had to leave at the age of 11, 12 or 13. It was the responsibility of the poor law union to find apprenticeships for the boys and places for the girls to go into service.

However, before the 1880s, the only record of children being sent into service may be a mention in the minute book of the Board of Guardians for a particular poor law union. This is particularly the case in areas outside the cities.

From the 1880s onwards, and earlier for London, poor law unions started to keep separate registers of children boarded out, apprenticed or sent into service. Such records may be called 'children's registers', 'apprenticeship books' or 'register of children in service'.

The workhouse or poorhouse might also figure in a servant's life during old age or illness. Admission and discharge records list inmates who had to seek relief in the workhouse or poorhouse. Large numbers of them were servants who had been unable to save for their old age, or who had fallen on hard times through being ill and unable to work.

Coverage of poor law union records varies across the country, with some areas having almost complete sets of records and others having none. Check A2A (www.a2a.org.uk) or the Scottish Archive Network (www.scan.org.uk).

Large numbers of records in the London Metropolitan Archives Poor Law Collection have been digitised and are available to view through Ancestry (www.ancestry.co.uk). They are not yet searchable by name but if you know the area of London in which your ancestor lived, you can browse the records of the corresponding poor law union. They are arranged into types of record, and the best ones to check are the children's registers or apprenticeship books. Some of the registers have a useful index at the front.

Chapter 13

SPECIFIC SOURCES FOR SERVANTS

Estate Records

If your ancestor was in service on a landed estate, it's well worth finding out if any relevant records have survived. In many cases, estate records are still held by the family which created them; in others, they have been deposited in a county record office or archive. You can find out by keying in the name of the estate into the 'advanced search' facility on Access to Archives (A2A) or the Scottish Archive Network for Scotland. Alternatively, simply contact the nearest archives to the estate as the staff will usually know of the whereabouts of any surviving records.

Bear in mind that your ancestor may not be mentioned in the records, simply because employment records have not survived, or because there are gaps in the coverage of the documents.

Estate records cover a large number of subjects and types of document, ranging from the landowner's personal diaries and correspondence, maps and floor plans, through to duties of staff and wages, livery and pension books. All can be useful for family history research.

Personal correspondence can reveal the opinions of the writer about a particular servant or domestic servants in general, and how he or she treated them. The Galton Papers, for example, is an archive of business and family correspondence of the Galton family, which is held at Birmingham Archives and Heritage Service. The Galtons lived at Dudson in Birmingham from the mid-eighteenth century and in this letter, the family's companion, Lucy Ann Patterson, is writing to John Howard Galton about the importance of maintaining discipline with the servants in the household. He had married Isabella Strutt the previous year:

27 January 1820

Your Drudge appears to me a man likely to be a valuable servant (if he is not spoilt by too much kindness & consideration). Mr Galton is so much pleased with his good sense that we are to look out for his counterpart for Dudson & if I find one it is upon condition that I am to . . . keep him in good order & take care that he does not relax in his industry & good Habits. I shall make a very rigid Master & I strongly recommend you to do likewise . . . it is but lately that I am become so Hard Hearted.

The family only has of late experience how true it is that a system of relaxed discipline is sure to produce relaxed Morals – thus we have lost several originally excellent Servants.

(MS 3101/C/D/10/61/63, Birmingham Archives and Heritage Service)

If maps of the estate have survived, they should show you the main house in its context with the gardens, workers' cottages, etc. Even more fascinating are floor plans of the house which will name each room, including the various sections of the servants' quarters. Some estate archives contain lists of duties for staff which can also reveal how much work your ancestor was expected to do.

Perhaps of most value to family historians are wages, livery and pension books. Wages were originally paid yearly or half yearly, although later in the nineteenth century quarterly pay became more usual. The books will name each servant (often with their job title), and will list the amount of salary paid. If your ancestor is included in a wages book, and he or she was there for some time, you will be able to see how they progressed in terms of promotions or increases in pay.

Receipts for wages may also be available; these were written out by the land agent (or whoever was in charge of paying the wages) and were signed by the servant, so there is a possibility you may see your ancestor's signature. Livery books record the items of clothing given to liveried servants such as footmen and coachmen; their wage is often also included.

For those workers who had retired from service, pensions were often granted, and these were sometimes transferred to widows once the husband had died. Upper servants usually received an annuity once or twice a year, while estate workers might have a weekly sum of money.

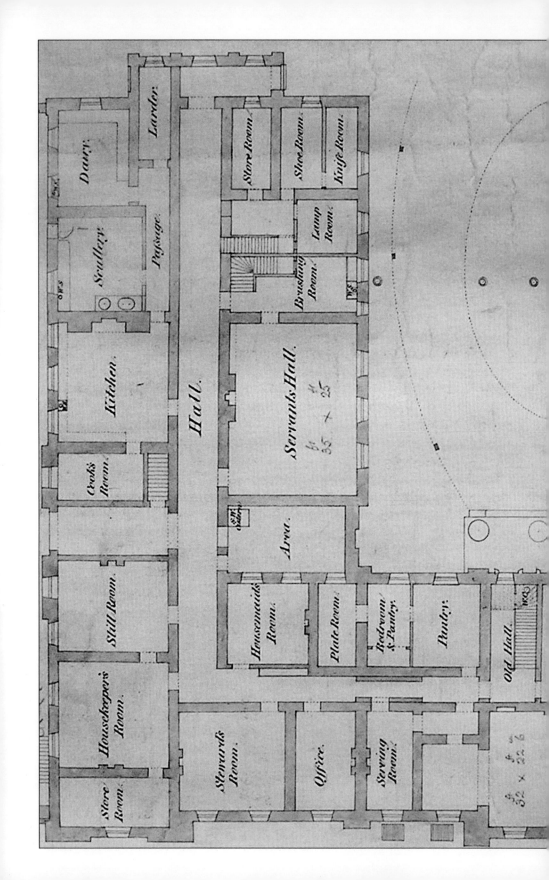

Larder.

Dairy.

Scullery.

Passage.

Store Room.

Shoe Room.

Knife Room.

Lamp Room.

Brushing Room.

Kitchen.

Cook's Room.

Hall.

Servants' Hall.

35 × 25

Still Room.

Area.

Housekeeper's Room.

Housemaids' Room.

Plate Room.

Bedroom & Pantry.

Pantry.

Old Hall.

Store Room.

Steward's Room.

Office.

Serving Room.

32 × 22

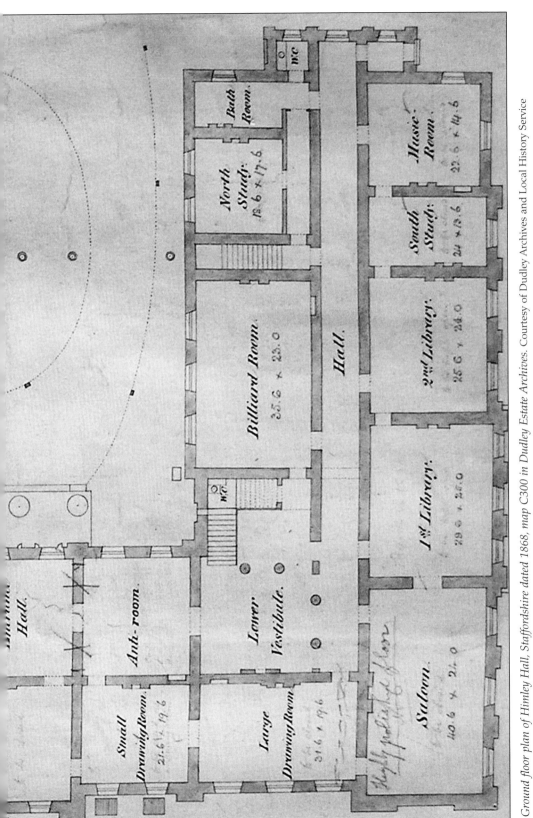

Ground floor plan of Himley Hall, Staffordshire dated 1868, map C300 in Dudley Estate Archives. Courtesy of Dudley Archives and Local History Service

Household Accounts

Many county record offices and archives hold household account books which have been deposited by private families who did not own a landed estate. These can be interesting to read since they may include duties of servants, and notes of when servants started or left, together with their wages. Search on A2A for England and Wales, or the Scottish Archive Network for Scotland to find out what's available.

Tax records

If your ancestor was in service in the late eighteenth century, tax records are another valuable source to check. Householders were liable to pay tax on their male servants from 1777, and a further tax on female servants was introduced in 1785, although this was repealed seven years later because it was so unpopular. The tax on male servants was not finally abolished until 1937. Taxes were collected by parish assessors; the survival of servants' tax returns varies across the country.

In Scotland, returns are available for male servants from 1777 to 1798 and for female servants from 1785 to 1792. They are held in the National Archives of Scotland in Edinburgh, catalogued under E326/5 for male servants and E326/6 for females. They list the name and address of the employer, the names of his servants, and often their precise occupation (under the 'Quality of Servants' column). The amount of tax to be paid is also included. You can see an example of a return for male servants in the county of Aberdeen on the Scottish Archive Network's Virtual Vault: http://www.scan.org.uk/researchrtools/tax.htm.

Unfortunately, the equivalent series of records for England and Wales has not survived. The National Archives holds an alphabetical list of persons who paid tax on male servants in 1780 (catalogued under T 47/8), together with the place and county in which they lived and the number of servants kept, but the document does not name any servants. The Society of Genealogists also holds a manuscript index to persons paying tax on male servants in 1780, but there is no similar index for those who employed female servants.

Nineteenth-century licences for male servants are frequently found in county record offices as part of a particular estate's archive or as a bundle of items from a household. However, they are not very useful for family history research (unless your ancestor was the employer) as they do not name the servant for which the licence was paid; they simply state how many were liable for tax.

A licence for male servants, carriages, armorial bearings . . . and dogs, granted to Richard Cripps Esquire, dated 26 January 1898. Author's collection

Charity Records

Supplementing the work of poor law unions were a large number of charitable organisations, which either placed girls in service or helped to improve their situations by offering support and advice. These have already been described in detail in Chapter 3: Who Went into Service?

An excellent introduction to the work of the Girls' Friendly Society can be found in an online exhibition entitled 'Bear ye one another's burdens': http://www.londonmet.ac.uk/thewomenslibrary/whats-on/exhibitions/gfs.cfm. The Women's Library at London Metropolitan University holds the bulk of the Girls' Friendly Society archive, while county record offices hold material relating to branches of the society. In some cases, this may include membership registers, although it is more usual to find annual reports, minute books and account books.

Annual reports of the Metropolitan Association for Befriending Young Servants (MABYS) still exist and some records survive of the reports made on girls in service who were being supervised by MABYS. These are held at the London Metropolitan Archives and can be found scattered amongst the records of the workhouses from which the girls were discharged. Some of these documents have been digitised as part of London Metropolitan Archives' Poor Law Collection and can be seen online through Ancestry (www.ancestry.co.uk).

The London Metropolitan Archives also holds the Foundling Hospital collection (catalogued under A/FH), which covers the years 1741–1979. Large numbers of the unmarried women who gave up their children to the care of the hospital were servants, and the information in the records provides tantalising details of their working life. The hospital also kept employment registration books for those children who were apprenticed out. Please note: as the documents contain information on named individuals, these registers are closed for 110 years from the last date in the document.

Barnardo's holds a huge archive of records about the children it cared for, dating back to the 1870s. It had training homes for girls, and placed large numbers of its female orphans in service. Archive staff will search the archive on your behalf for a fee; see the Useful Contacts section.

County record offices may also hold archives for local charitable organisations which assisted servants. Try searching on Access to Archives (www.a2a.org.uk) for England and Wales or the Scottish Archive Network (www.scan.org.uk).

Records of Government Training Schemes

While various charities and poor law institutions provided domestic training for girls and young women in the nineteenth and early twentieth centuries, the government set up its own training scheme between the First and Second World War. These specifically targeted areas of high unemployment, and material about the schemes can be found at the National Archives in the Ministry of Labour records collection. The names of some individual students are included.

Trade Union Records

If your ancestor was in service in the late nineteenth or early twentieth century, it is possible he or she was a member of one of the trade unions devoted to domestic workers. Material relating to the London and Provincial Domestic Servants' Union (established 1891) is in the National Archives, while the Modern Records Centre at the University of Warwick holds information on the National Domestic Workers' Union (founded 1919), the Domestic Workers' Guild (formed 1932) and the National Union of Domestic Workers (established 1938). Unfortunately, none of the available material includes information on members.

Diaries and Memoirs of Servants

Another extremely valuable source for finding out more about your ancestor's working life are the diaries of servants. They are, by their very nature, rare to find and, where they are available, they may have been written by upper servants. Lower servants had little time for such frivolities as writing a diary.

While it is highly unlikely you will find a diary written by your own ancestor, it is still possible to glean much detail from the diary entries of other servants who may have worked in similar roles, or who mention those fulfilling the same role as your ancestor.

The diaries of Hannah Cullwick are often quoted as a rare example of a journal kept by a housemaid/kitchen-maid. She wrote them at the instigation of Arthur Munby, a barrister and civil servant in the Ecclesiastical Commissioners' Office, whom she met in 1854. He had a strong interest in working-class women, and they had a clandestine relationship, marrying secretly in 1873.

Hannah's diary entries record her daily routine as a maid of all work in London, and her memoirs give details about her previous employment as a servant in country houses. The original diaries are held in the library of Trinity

College, Cambridge as part of the Munby Collection but there is a useful printed edition, edited by Elizabeth Stanley (see bibliography).

The diary of footman William Tayler (edited by Dorothy Wise) is extremely interesting because it gives an insight into his daily life and his thoughts about his employer and the other servants kept in the household. He worked in London for the wealthy widow Mrs Prinsep and her unmarried daughter. Born in 1807 in Oxfordshire, William Tayler kept a diary for the year 1837 'as I am a wretched bad writer [and] many of my friends have advised me to practice more ...'

On Sundays, he usually went to see his wife and children who were lodged nearby, although he never mentioned her or them by name. He was the only man-servant employed as the coachman was 'only a sort of jobber'. There were also three maidservants, who were 'very quiet good sort of bodys, and we live very comfortable together'. Two of Mrs Prinsep's sons were dead and 'their widows are often visiting here as well as some of the other sons' children – much oftner than we want them.'

In his first entry on 1 January 1837, he listed his daily duties:

I got up at half past seven, cleaned the boys' clothes and knives [and] lamps, got the parlour breakfast, lit my pantry fire, cleared breakfast and washed it away, dressed myself, went to church, came back, got parlour lunch, had my own dinner, sat by the fire and red [sic] the Penny Magazine and opened the door when any visitors came. At 4 o'clock had my tea, took the lamps and candles up into the drawing room, shut the shutters, took glass, knives, plate and settera into the dining room, layed [sic] the cloth for dinner, took the dinner up at six o'clock, waited at dinner, brought the things down again at seven, washed them up, brought down the desert [sic], got ready the tea, took it up at eight o'clock, brought it down at half past, washed up, had my supper at nine, took down the lamps and candles at half past ten and went to bed at eleven.

Despite his long list of daily duties, William was still able to find time for walking out, entertaining his own visitors and indulging his passion for drawing. He was paid 'forty two pounds pr. year, my victuals and drink and lodgings in the bargan [sic], besides all the perquisites I can make in such services as mine. These perquasites jenerally [sic] amount to about ten or fifteen pounds per. year more or less ...'

The servants at Mrs Prinsep's were well fed although almost all of them had to find their own tea and sugar. William's entry for 22 January records a typical day's meals:

> This day we had for dinner a piece of surloin of beef, roasted broccoli and potatos [sic] and preserved damson pie. We all have tea together at four o'clock with bread and butter and sometimes a cake. At nine o'clock we have supper; this evening it's cold beef and damson pie. We keep plenty of very good table ale at this house and every one can have as much as they like.

William's penultimate entry on 30 December 1837 was very poignant as it reflected on his occupation:

> The life of a gentleman's servant is something like that of a bird shut up in a cage. The bird is well housed and well fed but is deprived of liberty, and liberty is the dearest and sweetest object of all Englishmen . . . I would rather be like the sparrow or the lark, have less houseing [sic] and feeding and rather more liberty.

Memoirs and autobiographies of servants are also useful resources, although they are usually written many years after the event so they may not be as historically accurate as diaries. The most useful collections of autobiographies are in John Burnett's *Useful Toil: Autobiographies of Working People from the 1820s to the 1920s*, Margaret Llewelyn Davies's *Life As We Have Known It By Co-operative Working Women* and Noel Streatfeild's *The Day Before Yesterday: Firsthand Stories of Fifty Years Ago*. Eric Horne's *What the Butler Winked At* and Rosina Harrison's *My Life in Service* are also very interesting; see the bibliography for full information.

Records of Servants' Registry Offices

Where available, the records of servants' registry offices can provide information about the salaries paid to servants placed with them and the kind of conditions offered by the employers. As they were private businesses, the survival rate of such records is low, unless they have been lodged with the local record office. You can find out whether documents are available for a particular area by checking on A2A or the Scottish Archive Network for Scotland.

A small sample of the records of the Lightwoods registry are held at Birmingham Archives and Heritage Service. The registers record the name of the employer seeking a servant and her address; the type of servant and the wages offered; plus any other information likely to attract an applicant.

For example, in 1910, Mrs Roy was looking for a 'cook general' at between

£18 and £20 and a 'house parlourmaid' at between £16 and £18 a year. She was at pains to point out that there were '4 maids kept & man for boots'.

Miss Kemp of 232 Bristol Road, Edgbaston also wanted a 'cook general' and was prepared to pay between £18 and £20. Her offer was 'Family three, early dinners, two men kept, no washing'. Meanwhile, Mrs Marsh of 'Elmdene', Little Moor Hill, Smethwick wanted a 20-year-old general servant at between £12 and £14. Although there were seven in the family, she added that the servant would have 'every Sunday out' and a 'good home'. (MS 1437/1, Birmingham Archives and Heritage Service)

Contemporary Household Management Manuals

In the nineteenth century, a plethora of household management manuals were published with the middle-classes as their target readership. These books can be extremely useful as they give details of suggested duties for various servants and recommended wages. However, these manuals were aspirational and were not taken literally by their readers, nor should they be used in this way to gain background information on your ancestor's working life.

Google Books is an excellent online source of household management manuals (books.google.com). When you have found a book you're interested in, if it offers a 'full view' instead of 'snippet view', you can view the whole book as a PDF and then use the 'find' facility to search for particular words e.g. housemaids, wages etc. Here are a few suggestions:

Samuel and Sarah Adams, *The Complete Servant* (1825)
Mrs Isabella Beeton, *Book of Household Management* (1861)
Mrs Florence Caddy, *Household Organisation* (1877)
Mrs J E Panton, *From Kitchen to Garret* (1888)
Anon., *The Servants' Practical Guide* (1880)

Many of these household management manuals are being reprinted by publishers on a 'print on demand' basis – in these instances, Google Books will not allow a 'full view' of the book.

Appendix 1

USEFUL CONTACTS

Access to Archives (A2A)
www.a2a.org.uk

Barnardo's Family History Service
www.barnardos.org.uk

British Library Newspapers, Colindale, London
Tel: 020 7412 7353
www.bl.uk

Leeds District Probate Registry
Tel: 0113 389 6133
www.justice.gov.uk/guidance/courts-and-tribunals/courts/probate/family-history.htm

London Metropolitan Archives
Tel: 020 7332 3820
www.cityoflondon.gov.uk/Corporation/LGNL_Services/Leisure_and_culture/Records_and_archives

Mitchell Library, Glasgow
Tel: 0141 287 2910
www.mitchelllibrary.org/virtualmitchell

Modern Records Centre, University of Warwick
Tel: 024 7652 4219
www2.warwick.ac.uk/services/library/mrc

Munby Collection, Trinity College, Cambridge
Tel: 01223 333122
www.lib.cam.ac.uk/deptserv/rarebooks/directory.html

National Archives of Scotland, Edinburgh
Tel: 0131 535 1314
www.nas.gov.uk

Scottish Archive Network
www.scan.org.uk

The National Archives, Kew
Tel: 020 8876 3444
www.nationalarchives.gov.uk

The Society of Genealogists, London
Tel: 020 7251 8799
www.sog.org.uk

The Women's Library, London Metropolitan University
Tel: 020 7320 2222
www.londonmet.ac.uk/thewomenslibrary

Appendix 2

PLACES TO VISIT

There are lots of former stately homes, now run by the National Trust, English Heritage or other organisations, which have servants' quarters you can visit. Here is a small selection:

Properties run by the National Trust
Tel: 0844 800 1895
www.nationaltrust.org.uk

Berrington Hall, Leominster
Blickling Hall, Norfolk
Calke Abbey, Derbyshire
Carlyle's House, London (a small middle-class house with servants' quarters in the kitchen and attic)
Castle Coole, County Fermanagh
Castle Drogo, Devon
Castle Ward, County Down
Cotehele, Cornwall
Cragside, Northumberland
Dinefewr Park and Castle, Carmarthenshire
Dunham Massey, Altrincham, Cheshire
Erddig Hall, Wrexham
Ickworth House, Suffolk
Knole, Kent
Lanhydrock, Cornwall
Llanerchaeron, Ceredigion
Nostell Priory House, West Yorkshire
Penrhyn Castle, Gwynedd
Petworth House, West Sussex
Shugborough Estate, Staffordshire
Speke Hall, Liverpool
Tatton Park, Cheshire

Treasurer's House, York
Uppark House and Garden, West Sussex
Wimpole Hall, Cambridgeshire

Properties run by The National Trust for Scotland
Tel: 0844 493 2100
www.nts.org.uk

Hill of Tarvit Mansionhouse and Garden, Fife
Pollok House, Glasgow

Properties run by English Heritage
Tel: 0870 333 1181
www.english-heritage.org.uk

Audley End House and Gardens, Essex
Brodsworth Hall and Gardens, South Yorkshire

Properties run by other organisations
Bramall Hall, Greater Manchester
Tel: 0161 485 3708
www.bramallhall.org

Christchurch Mansion, Ipswich
Tel: 01473 433554
www.ipswich.gov.uk/site/scripts/documents_info.php?documentID=691

Harewood House, Leeds
Tel: 0113 218 1010
www.harewood.org

Lauriston Castle, Edinburgh
Tel: 0131 336 2060
www.edinburgh.gov.uk/directory_record/5047/lauriston_castle

Manderston, Duns, Berwickshire
Tel: 01361 882 636
www.manderston.co.uk

Preston Manor, Sussex
Tel: 03000 290900
www.brighton-hove-rpml.org.uk/Museums/prestonmanor/Pages/home.aspx

Stansted Park, Hampshire
Tel: 023 9241 2265
www.stanstedpark.co.uk

Thirlestane Castle, Lauder, Scottish Borders
Tel: 01578 722430
www.thirlestanecastle.co.uk

Tredegar House, Newport
Tel: 01633 815880
www.newport.gov.uk/_dc/index.cfm?fuseaction=thingstosee.tredegarhouse

BIBLIOGRAPHY

Adams, Samuel and Sarah, *The Complete Servant* (Southover Press, 1989)

Aitchison, Jean, *Servants in Ayrshire 1750–1914* (Ayrshire Archaeological and Natural History Society, 2001)

Aitken, James (ed.), *English Diaries of the Nineteenth Century* (Pelican Books, 1944)

Anon., *The Servants' Practical Guide* (1880)

Beeton, Mrs Isabella, *The Book of Household Management* (S O Beeton Publishing, 1861)

Best, Geoffrey, *Mid-Victorian Britain 1851–1875* (Fontana Press, 1979)

Booth, Charles (ed.), *Life and Labour of the People of London: Volume VIII: Population Classified by Trades* (Macmillan & Co, 1896)

Bridgeman, Harriet and Drury, Elizabeth, *Victorian Household Hints* (Adam and Charles Black Publishers Ltd, 1981)

Burnett, John (ed.), *Useful Toil: Autobiographies of Working People from the 1820s to the 1920s* (Routledge, 1994)

Collet, Miss, *Report on the Money Wages of Indoor Domestic Servants* (Board of Trade, 1899)

Davies, Margaret Llewelyn (ed.), *Life As We Have Known It, By Co-operative Working Women* (Virago Press, 1977)

Dawes, Frank Victor, *Not in Front of the Servants: A True Portrait of Upstairs, Downstairs Life* (Wayland, 1973)

Flanders, Judith, *The Victorian House* (HarperCollins, 2003)

George, M Dorothy, *London Life in the Eighteenth Century* (Peregrine Books, 1966)

Hackwood, Frederick Wm, *A History of West Bromwich* (Brewin Books, 2001 reprint)

Harrison, J F C, *Early Victorian Britain 1832–1851* (Fontana Press, 1988)

Harrison, J F C, *Late Victorian Britain 1875–1901* (Fontana Press, 1990)

Harrison, Rosina, *Rose: My Life in Service* (Cassell & Company Limited, 1975)

Hayward, Edward, *Upstairs and Downstairs: Life in an English Country House* (Pitkin Unichrome Ltd, 1998)

Horn, Pamela, *Flunkeys and Scullions: Life Below Stairs in Georgian England* (The History Press, 2004)

Horn, Pamela, *Life Below Stairs in the Twentieth Century* (Sutton Publishing, 2001)

Horn, Pamela, *My Ancestor was in Service: A Guide to Sources for Family Historians* (Society of Genealogists, 2009)

Horn, Pamela, *The Rise and Fall of the Victorian Servant* (Alan Sutton Publishing, 1986)

Horne, Eric, *What the Butler Winked At: Being the Life and Adventures of Eric Horne, Butler* (T. Werner Laurie, 1923)

Hughes, M V, *A London Home in the 1890s* (Oxford University Press, 1946)

King, Ernest, *Green Baize Door* (William Kimber, 1963)

Marshall, Dorothy, *The English Domestic Servant in History* (Historical Association, 1949)

Mason, Shena, *The Hardware Man's Daughter: Matthew Boulton and his 'Dear Girl'* (Phillimore, 2005)

Mason, Shena, *Soho House Guide* (BM&AG, 2002)

May, Trevor, *The Victorian Domestic Servant* (Shire Publications, 2007)

Mitchell, R J and Leys, M D R, *A History of London Life* (Penguin Books 1968)

Musson, Jeremy, *Up and Down Stairs: The History of the Country House Servant* (John Murray Publishers, 2009)

Panton, Jane Ellen, *From Kitchen to Garret: Hints to Young Householders* (Ward & Downey, 1888)

Pepys, Samuel, *The Diary of Samuel Pepys* (J M Dent and Sons Limited, 1924)

Powell, Margaret, *Below Stairs* (Pan Books, 1970)

Radmore, David F, *Himley Hall and Park: A History* (Dudley Libraries, 1996)

Rennie, Jean, *Every Other Sunday: The Autobiography of a Kitchen-maid* (Arthur Barker, 1955)

Royston Pike, E, *Human Documents of the Age of the Forsytes* (George Allen & Unwin Ltd, 1969)

Royston Pike, E, *Human Documents of the Victorian Golden Age* (George Allen & Unwin Ltd, 1967)

Sambrook, Pamela, *Keeping Their Place: Domestic Service in the Country House* (Sutton Publishing, 2005)

Scott-Moncrieff, M C, *Yes, Ma'am! Glimpses of Domestic Service 1901–1951* (Albyn Press Ltd, 1984)

Stanley, Elizabeth (ed.), *The Diaries of Hannah Cullwick: Victorian Maidservant* (Virago Press, 1984)

Streatfeild, Noel (ed.), *The Day Before Yesterday: Firsthand Stories of Fifty Years Ago* (Collins, 1956)

Stuart Macrae, Mrs (ed.), *Cassell's Household Guide: A Complete Cyclopaedia of*

Domestic Economy (The Waverley Book Company, 1911)

Trollope, Anthony, *The Last Chronicle of Barset* (1867)

Turner, E S, *What the Butler Saw: Two Hundred and Fifty Years of the Servant Problem* (Michael Joseph Ltd., 1962)

Vickery, Amanda, *The Gentlemen's Daughter: Women's Lives in Georgian England* (Yale University Press, 1999)

Waterson, Merlin, *The Servants' Hall: The Domestic History of a Country House*, (The National Trust, 1990)

Williams, E N, *Life in Georgian England* (B T Batsford Ltd, 1962)

Wise, Dorothy (ed.), *Diary of William Tayler, Footman 1837* (St. Marylebone Society, 1987)

Woodforde, James, *A Country Parson: James Woodforde's Diary 1759–1802* (Century Publishing and Oxford University Press, 1985)

Articles in Periodicals

Agnew, Lady, 'Ten Thousand A Year', in *Cornhill Magazine*, August 1901

Boucherett, Jessie, 'Legislative Restrictions on Women's Labour', in *Englishwoman's Review*, 1873

Colmore, G, 'Eight Hundred A Year', in *Cornhill Magazine*, June 1901

Dickens, Charles, 'No Hospital for Incurables', in *Household Words* (24 August 1850)

Dickens, Charles, 'London's Pauper Children', in *Household Words* (31 August 1850)

Earle, Mrs, 'Eighteen Hundred A Year', in *Cornhill Magazine*, July 1901

Marris, N Murrell, 'Servant London', in *Living London*, 1902 (Volume 2, pp 351–7)

Martineau, Harriet, 'Modern Domestic Service', in *Edinburgh Review*, April 1862 (pp 409–39)

Millin, George F, 'London Servants: High and Low', in *English Illustrated Magazine*, June 1894 (pp 939–47)

Periodicals and Newspapers

Cornhill Magazine
Edinburgh Review
English Illustrated Magazine
Englishwoman's Review
Household Words
Living London

Pall Mall Gazette
Punch
The Graphic
The Illustrated London News
The Times

Websites

Jackson, Lee: The Victorian Dictionary, www.victorianlondon.org

Richmond, Vivienne, 'Bear Ye One Another's Burdens: The Girls' Friendly Society 1875–2005' (online exhibition), www.londonmet.ac.uk/thewomens library/gfs/gfs_home.html

The National Archives Currency Converter, www.nationalarchives.gov.uk/currency

INDEX